QUILTING
Through the Year

16 Delightful Designs for Every Season

SHERILYN MORTENSEN

Landauer Publishing

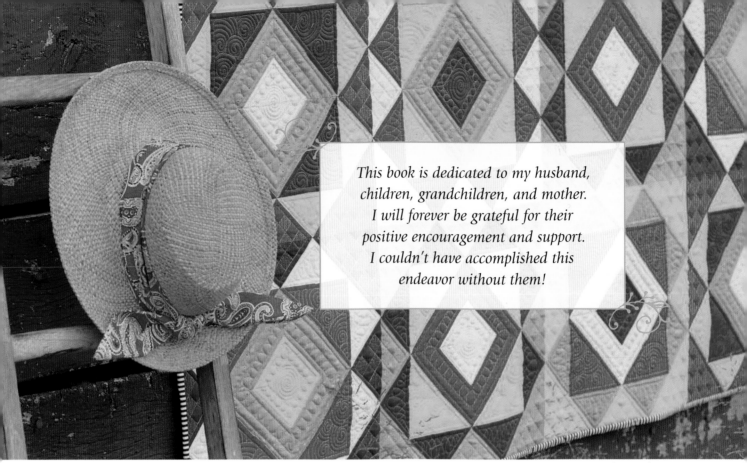

This book is dedicated to my husband, children, grandchildren, and mother. I will forever be grateful for their positive encouragement and support. I couldn't have accomplished this endeavor without them!

Freedom quilt, see page 56

Quilting Through the Year

Landauer Publishing, www.landauerpub.com, is an imprint of Fox Chapel Publishing Company, Inc.

Project Team
Editors: Amelia Johanson and Jodi Butler
Copy Editor: Sherry Vitolo
Designer: Wendy Reynolds
Illustrators: Sue Friend and Kerry Bogert
Photographers: Jennifer Tarkington (beauty shots), Sherilyn Mortensen (all other photography)

ISBN: 978-1-947163-69-0

Library of Congress Control Number: 2021943159

We are always looking for talented authors. To submit an idea, please send a brief inquiry to acquisitions@foxchapelpublishing.com.

Note to Professional Copy Services:
The publisher grants you permission to make up to six copies of any quilt patterns in this book for any customer who purchased this book and states the copies are for personal use.

Printed in the United States of America
24 23 22 21 2 4 6 8 10 9 7 5 3 1

This book has been published with the intent to provide accurate and authoritative information in regard to the subject matter within. While every precaution has been taken in the preparation of this book, the author and publisher expressly disclaim any responsibility for any errors, omissions, or adverse effects arising from the use or application of the information contained herein.

Introduction

I love quilting for every season, which is what inspired me to write this book. In *Quilting Through the Year*, you'll find a collection of 16 fun and creative designs with projects for winter, spring, summer, and fall. Whether you're looking for a pattern to add seasonal charm to your own home or sewing a gift for a friend or loved one, these beginner-friendly quilt projects boast charming motifs that you will want to return to again and again.

Each project, from throws and table toppers to wall hangings and full-sized quilts, is created with traditionally cut geometric pieces—no circles or curves—that are achievable for quilters of every skill level. Yet the visuals give the illusion of curves without the challenge of sewing them. Smaller motifs are often repeated, so once you've made one block, the process is a snap to master. Other designs piece together shapes in different ways to create unique figures. From a scarfed snowman to a gorgeous daisy field, these designs capture the most beloved features of every season in a truly delightful way that will make you want to harness the joy of the season with fabric and thread.

Sherilyn

The author in her studio.

Summer's Delight quilt, see page 46

Follow the Sun quilt, see page 60

Contents

14

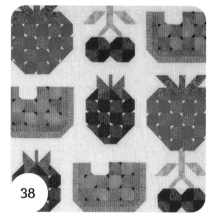

38

60

86

20

30

34

46

52

56

66

72

80

92

100

108

Quilting Basics

Tools

SEWING MACHINE WITH A ¼" (0.6CM) FOOT
All of the projects in this book can be made with a sewing machine with a ¼" (0.6cm) quilting foot and basic straight-line sewing capabilities. Use a scant ¼" (0.6cm) seam allowance for piecing all of the quilts.

HIGH-QUALITY THREAD
Using a high-quality 50wt cotton thread or cotton-covered polyester thread for piecing makes a big difference in the look and integrity of your quilting projects. White, cream, or light gray are good neutral colors that usually blend well with most fabrics. Superior Threads and Aurifil are my favorite brands.

SCISSORS
Proper cutting is key with quilting. I highly recommend investing in a pair of good-quality sewing scissors and little snips, which come in handy when sewing. Kai is my brand of choice.

STRAIGHT PINS
I like to use long, thin straight pins for quilting and sewing. Fortunately, there are many great brands to choose from, so you can choose the ones that work best for you.

IRON
Pressing seam allowances as you work helps prevent little bits of fabric from getting "lost" within seam allowances, which can create distortions and make your finished quilt blocks smaller than they should be. Additionally, careful pressing can also save time when assembling your quilt because the blocks will fit together as they should. Use a quality steam iron, preferably cordless.

IRONING BOARD/MAT
A basic ironing board or mat is sufficient for quilting and sewing. I like the convenience of using a large wool ironing mat.

SPRAY STARCH
Spray starch helps seams and quilt blocks lay flatter, and can add a little stiffness to your fabric. Best Press or Flatter Brands make great spray starches. Tip: Try to avoid starches with color dyes, which can run.

STRAIGHT EDGE QUILTING RULERS
As I previously mentioned, proper cutting is key for quilting. I like to use rulers that are 5" x 15" (12.7cm x 38.1cm) or larger, preferably from Missouri Star Quilt Co.

QUILTING SQUARE-UP RULERS
These rulers are ideal for helping you make perfect squares. Use a square-up ruler that's 6" (15.2cm) or larger. Sew Square Rulers by Sew Kind of Wonderful are my first choice.

ROTARY CUTTER & CUTTING MAT
My favorite rotary cutter is the OLFA 45mm Ergonomic Rotary Cutter-RTY-2/DX paired with the Gypsy brand Rotary Blade Guards. It is available from Checker Distributors and helps me cut perfectly straight lines every time and avoid cut fingers. Use a 17" x 23" (43.2cm x 58.4cm) cutting mat or larger for trimming blocks and more.

The Robin Egg Blue quilt uses half square triangles and corner flip units to create the illusion of curved pieces.

Half Square Triangles

Half Square Triangles (HSTs) are one of the most common and versatile quilting blocks. They can be used on their own or as a foundation for more complicated designs. HSTs are used extensively throughout this book. To make a pair, you will need (2) fabric squares in different fabrics that are the exact same size.

1. Draw a diagonal line from corner to corner on the wrong side of one fabric square. Place one square on top of the other with right sides together and edges aligned. Pin the squares together, then sew along both sides of the drawn line with a ¼" (6mm) seam allowance.

 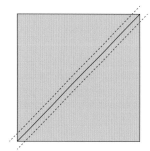

2. Rotary cut the square in half along the diagonal line. Open the HST units and press the seams open.

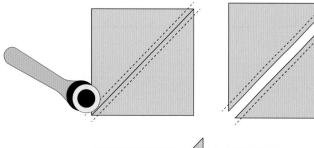

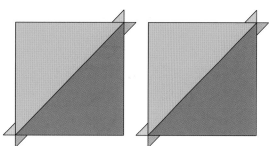

3. To square an HST, place a square-up ruler on the HST, centering the diagonal line on the ruler with the diagonal seam on the HST. If you are trimming the HST to 3½" (8.9cm) square, for example, make sure the fabric extends beyond the 3½" (8.9cm) marks on the ruler (indicated by bold red lines) and the edge of the ruler. Trim the fabric along the right side and top edge of the ruler.

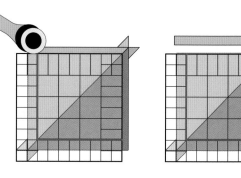

4. Turn the unit 180 degrees and place the ruler on top of the HST, aligning the trimmed edges with the "square-up dimensions." If you are trimming the HST to 3½" (8.9cm) square, for example, line up the trimmed edges directly under the 3½" (8.9cm) lines on the ruler and rotary cut the remaining edges of the HST.

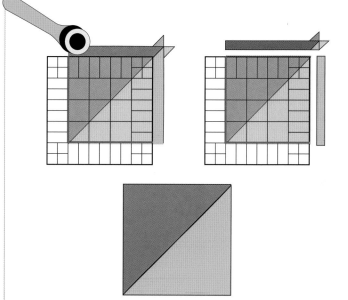

Quarter Half Square Triangles

To make a Quarter Half Square Triangle (QHST) you will need (1) Half Square Triangle (not squared) and (1) fabric square (follow the dimensions indicated in the pattern).

1. Using an erasable marking pencil, draw a diagonal line on the wrong side of the HST. Place the Half Square Triangle (HST) and fabric square right sides together (RST) with the HST on top. Sew along both sides of the drawn line with a ¼" (6mm) seam allowance.

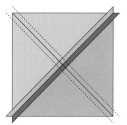
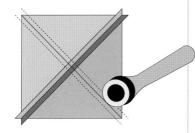

2. Rotary cut along the drawn line, resulting in (2) QHST units. Press the seams open. Note: Either one or both of the QHST units may be used, depending on the pattern. If only one of the QHST units is used, make sure it is the correct unit as indicated in the pattern.

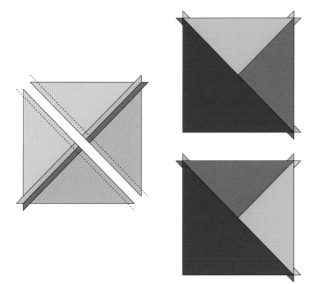

3. To square the QHST units to the dimensions indicated in the pattern, place a square-up ruler on the unit, centering the diagonal line on the ruler with the diagonal seam on the QHST. Make sure the fabric extends beyond the square-up dimensions (indicated by bold blue lines) and the edge of the ruler. Also, make sure the quarter triangle seam is directly under the square-up dimension number. If the QHST unit is being squared to 2½" (6.4cm), for example, make sure there is fabric beyond the 2½" (6.4cm) bold blue marks on the ruler and the edge of the ruler and that the quarter triangle seam is directly under the 2½" (6.4cm) mark on the ruler. Trim along the right side and top edge of the unit.

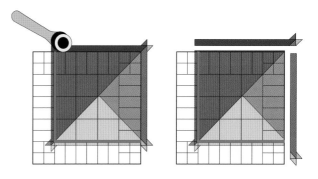

4. Turn the QHST unit 180 degrees and place the ruler on top of the unit, aligning the trimmed edges with the "square-up dimensions." For example, if squaring a QHST to 2½" (6.4cm) square, line up the trimmed edges directly under the 2½" (6.4cm) lines on the ruler. Trim along the remaining right side and top edges of block. Note: Both QHST units are squared the same way.

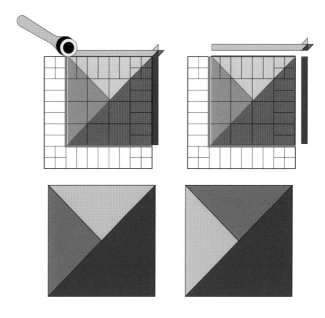

Corner Flip Units

Use this technique to make this common block feature. You will need two pieces for the "corner flip" technique. The dimensions can be found in the pattern you are following. In general, a smaller square is used to "corner flip" a larger square or rectangle corner.

1. Draw a diagonal line from corner to corner on the wrong side of the smaller fabric square.

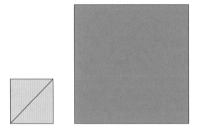

2. With right sides together and the drawn line showing, place the square on the corner of the larger piece of fabric, taking care to align the edges.

3. Stitch directly on the drawn line, then trim the fabric ¼" (6mm) from the stitch line.

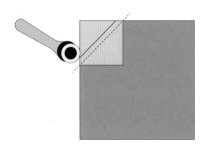 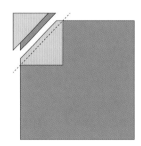

4. Flip the attached corner over and press the seam open.

Binding Quilt Edges

Each of the projects in this book calls for binding. Here is a method for doing just that. For a doubled binding, cut strips four times the width of the finished binding, plus ⅛–¼" (3–6mm) to accommodate the density of the quilt. Note: You can trim away batting and backing before stitching the binding to the quilt edge, or after.

1. Fold the binding strip lengthwise in half. With raw edges aligned, start stitching your binding, to the quilt edge, beginning on one side and leaving at least 5" (12.7cm) of unstitched binding as a tail. As you approach the corner, stop stitching ½" (1.3cm) before you reach the edge (if your binding is ¼" [6mm] wide, stop ¼" [6mm] from the edge). Backstitch or secure. Fold the binding up at a 90-degree angle.

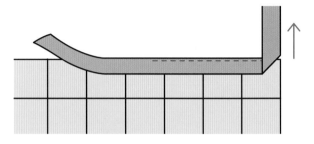

2. Then fold the binding back down so the raw edge of the binding is flush with the raw edge of the quilt/mat, and the top fold is aligned with the original side. Begin stitching where you left off on the previous side, making sure to fix your stitch line at the starting point. Continue around the quilt stopping approximately 7–8" (17.8–20.3cm) from your starting point.

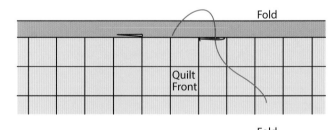
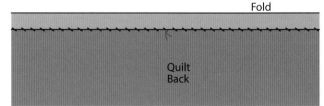

3. Place the tails smooth and flat along the quilt edge. The overlap will need to be the same amount as the width of your binding. For a 2¼" (5.7cm) binding, overlay 2⅛" (5.4cm). Clip the excess ends of the tails perpendicular to the edge of the mat.

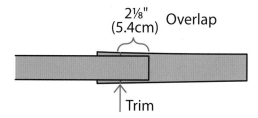

4. Place the ends right sides together at right angles. Stitch a diagonal line from corner to corner, and trim off the corner leaving a ¼" (6mm) seam allowance.

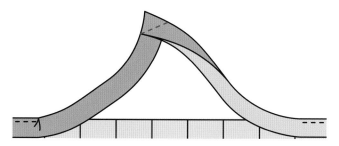

5. Finger press the binding into its original folded shape along the remaining raw edge of the quilt. Press, pin and continue stitching to secure, fixing your stitching line as you start and stop. If you have not trimmed away batting and backing, do so at this step.

6. Press the binding away from the front edge and fold over to the back of the quilt. Miter the binding at the corner and hand whipstitch into place with a single thread.

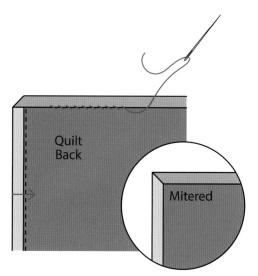

Joining Binding Ends

1. Join binding strips by overlapping the end of one strip perpendicular and right side together with the end of a second strip; you should have an upside L shape.

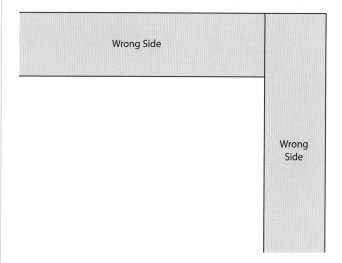

2. Stitch a diagonal seam from the left corner to the right corner of the overlap. Trim the seam allowance to ¼" (6mm) with a pinking sheer, and press the seam allowance open. Tip: Drawing a line from corner to corner with a wash-away marking pen or a light pencil, helps to keep your stitching in line.

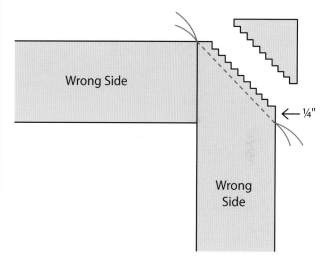

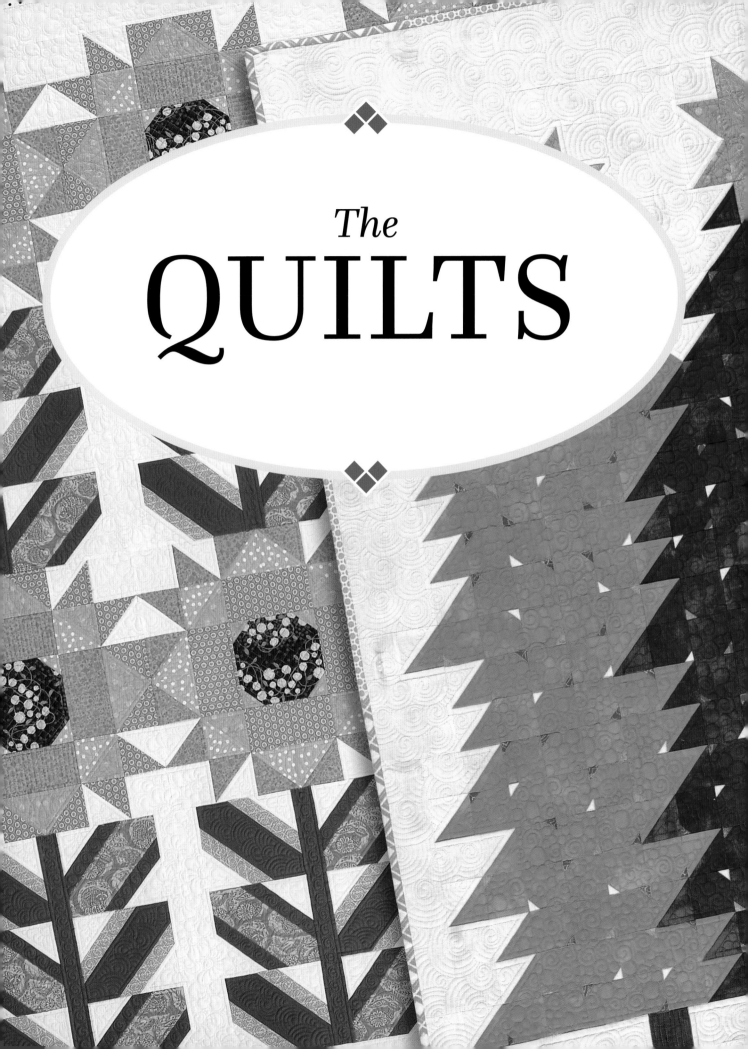

The
QUILTS

Robin Egg Blue

Seeing robins appear in early spring always gives me hope that warmer weather is coming soon. These two large robins proudly facing their adorable chicks and iconic blue eggs are a joyful reminder of spring's promise of new life and warmer days. This four-block mini quilt is the perfect size for a wall hanging or table topper.

36" (91.4cm) square
Designed, pieced, and quilted by Sherilyn Mortensen
Quilt bound by Amy Maxfield
Fabric: Paintbox basics by Elizabeth Hartman for Robert Kaufman, Moda Grunge

Fabric Requirements
- ⅓ yard (0.3m) Gray
- ¼ yard (0.2m) each Brown and Burnt Orange
- 2" x 10" (5.1cm x 25.4cm) Orange
- 2" (5.1cm) x Width of Fabric (WOF) or (1) 10" (25.4cm) square Black
- 3" (7.6cm) x WOF Yellow
- 9" x 28" (22.9cm x 71.1cm) Tan
- 4" x 12" (10.2 x 30.5cm) Turquoise
- 4" x 15" (10.2cm x 38.1cm) Aqua
- 1¼ yards (1.1m) White Background fabric
- 2½ yards (2.3m) Backing fabric
- ⅓ yard (0.3m) Binding fabric

Cutting Instructions

From Gray fabric (bird bodies), cut:
- (4) 3½" (8.9cm) squares
- (2) 2" x 6½" (5.1cm x 16.5cm) rectangles
- (6) 2" (5.1cm) squares
- (7) 4½" (11.4cm) squares
- (1) 3" (7.6cm) square

From Brown fabric (bird wings), cut:
- (2) 3½" x 6½" (8.9cm x 16.5cm) rectangles
- (3) 4½" (11.4cm) squares

From Burnt Orange fabric (bird chests), cut:
- (2) 4½" (11.4cm) squares
- (2) 3½" (8.9cm) squares
- (2) 2" x 6½" (5.1cm x 16.5cm) rectangles
- (1) 3" (7.6cm) square

From Orange fabric (chick beaks), cut:
- (6) 1¼" (3.2cm) squares

From Black fabric (bird eyes/legs), cut:
- (4) 1¼" (3.2cm) squares
- (4) 1¼" x 3½" (3.2cm x 8.9cm) squares

From Yellow fabric (chicks), cut:
- (4) 2" x 3½" (5.1cm x 8.9cm) rectangles
- (2) 2" x 2¾" (5.1cm x 7cm) rectangles
- (2) 1¼" x 2" (3.2cm x 5.1cm) rectangles
- (8) 1¼" (3.2cm) squares
- (2) 2" (5.1cm) squares

From Tan fabric (nests), cut:
- (2) 8" x 12½" (20.3cm x 31.8cm) rectangles

From Turquoise fabric (eggs/hatched eggs), cut:
- (2) 3½" (8.9cm) squares
- (4) 2" (5.1cm) squares

From Aqua fabric (eggs), cut:
- (4) 3½" (8.9cm) squares

From White Background fabric, cut:
- (2) 6½" x 9½" (16.5cm x 24.1cm) rectangles
- (4) 3½" x 9½" (8.9cm x 24.1cm) rectangles
- (2) 2" x 3½" (5.1cm x 8.9cm) rectangles
- (4) 3½" x 8" (8.9cm x 20.3cm) rectangles
- (4) 3½" x 18½" (8.9cm x 47cm) rectangles
- (2) 2" x 12½" (5.1cm x 31.8cm) rectangles
- (6) 3½" x 6½" (8.9cm x 16.5cm) rectangles
- (10) 3½" (8.9cm) squares
- (6) 4½" (11.4cm) squares
- (22) 1¼" (3.2cm) squares

Bird Block

Block size: 18½" (47cm) square (Make 2)
Make one right- and one left-facing Bird Block referring to the Bird Block Assembly diagrams throughout assembly. Press as desired unless otherwise directed, taking care to nest the seams by pressing in alternating directions. Note: Seams that don't need nesting can be pressed in either direction.

UNIT ASSEMBLY

1. Following the Half Square Triangle (HST) instructions on page 8, make the following HST units from 4½" (11.4cm) squares. Press and trim each unit to 3½" (8.9cm) square.
- (8) Gray/White units from (4) squares each
- (4) Gray/Brown units from (2) squares each
- (2) Brown/White units from (1) square each
- (2) Gray/Burnt Orange units from (1) square each
- (2) Burnt Orange/White units from (1) square each
  In the same manner, make (2) 2" (5.1cm) Gray/Burnt Orange HST units from (1) 3" (7.6cm) square each Gray and Burnt Orange for the neck. Trim to 2" (5.1cm) square.

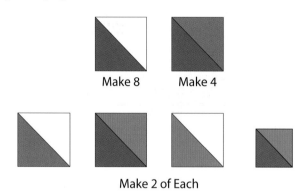

Make 8   Make 4

Make 2 of Each

2. Following the Corner Flip (CF) instructions on page 10, sew (1) 2" (5.1cm) Yellow square on the corner of (1) 3½" (8.9cm) White square. Make (2) beak units, pressing the seams open. In the same manner, sew (1) 1¼" (3.2cm) Black square on one corner of (1) 2" (5.1cm) Gray square. Make (2) eye units, pressing the seams open.

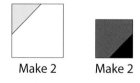

Make 2   Make 2

BIRD BLOCK ASSEMBLY
Each block uses:
- (1) 3½" (8.9cm) Burnt Orange/White HST unit
- (1) 3½" (8.9cm) Gray/Burnt Orange HST unit
- (4) 3½" (8.9cm) Gray/White HST units
- (1) 3½" (8.9cm) Brown/White HST unit
- (2) 3½" (8.9cm) Gray/Brown HST units
- (1) 2" (5.4cm) Gray/Burnt Orange HST unit
- (1) 3½" (8.9cm) White BG/Yellow CF unit (beak)
- (1) 2" (5.4cm) Gray/Black CF unit (eye)
- (1) 3½" x 6½" (8.9cm x 16.5cm) Gray/Burnt Orange strip set CF unit (as shown in step 4)
- (2) 2" (5.1cm) Gray squares
- (1) 3½" x 6½" (8.9cm x 16.5cm) Brown rectangle
- (2) 3½" (8.9cm) Gray squares
- (2) 1¼" x 3½" (3.2cm x 8.9cm) Black rectangles (legs)
- (1) 2" x 3½" (5.1cm x 8.9cm) White rectangle
- (1) 3½" (8.9cm) White square
- (2) 3½" x 8" (8.9cm x 20.3cm) White rectangles
- (2) 3½" x 9½" (8.9cm x 24.1cm) White rectangles
- (1) 6½" x 9½" (16.5cm x 24.1cm) White rectangle

1. Refer to the Right-Facing Bird Block Assembly Diagram throughout assembly. Make a four patch unit from (1) 2" (5.4cm) Gray/Black CF eye unit, (2) 2" (5.1cm) Gray squares, and (1) 2" (5.4cm) Gray/Burnt Orange HST as shown. Sew (1) 3½" (8.9cm) White/Yellow CF beak unit to the right side of the four patch unit and (1) 3½" (8.9cm) Gray/White HST to the left. Join (1) 3½" x 9½" (8.9cm x 24.1cm) White rectangle to the top of the unit you just made, then sew (1) 6½" x 9½" (16.5cm x 24.1cm) White rectangle on the left side.

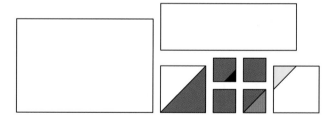

2. Join (1) 3½" (8.9cm) Gray square, (3) 3½" (8.9cm) Gray/White HST units, (1) 3½" (8.9cm) Gray/Brown HST unit, and (1) 3½" (8.9cm) White square as shown.

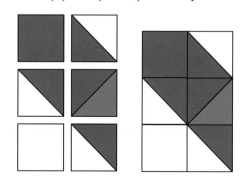

3. Join (1) 3½" (8.9cm) Brown/White HST unit and (1) 3½" (8.9cm) Gray/Brown HST unit with brown sides facing as shown. Sew (1) 3½" x 6½" (8.9cm x 16.5cm) Brown rectangle to the bottom of the HST unit. Join (1) 3½" (8.9cm) Gray/Burnt Orange HST unit and (1) 3½" (8.9cm) Gray square; sew to the bottom of the brown rectangle.

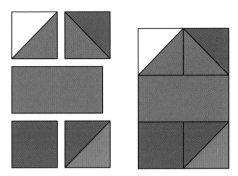

4. Join (1) 2" x 6½" (5.1cm x 16.5cm) rectangle each of Gray and Burnt Orange; press seams open. Make 2 Gray/Burnt Orange strip sets (one for each bird). Note: the Burnt Orange strip is the bird's chest and should be on the outer edge.

Following the CF directions on page 10 and referring to the diagram for placement, sew (1) 3½" (8.9cm) Burnt Orange square to the bottom right corner of a strip set for the right-facing bird and the bottom left corner of a strip set for the left-facing bird. Sew (1) Burnt Orange/White HST unit to the bottom of the CF unit as shown and (1) 3½" x 9½" (8.9cm x 24.1cm) White rectangle to the right side.

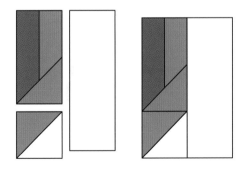

5. Join (2) 3½" x 8" (8.9cm x 20.3cm) White rectangles, (2) 1¼" x 3½" (3.2cm x 8.9cm) Black rectangles, and (1) 2" x 3½" (5.1cm x 8.9cm) White rectangle.

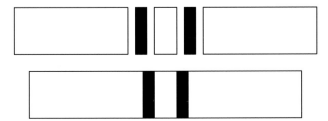

6. Join the sections together to complete the right-facing Bird Block. Trim to 18½" (47cm) square.

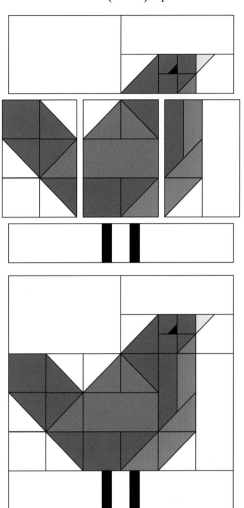

Right-Facing Bird Block Assembly Diagram

7. In the same manner, make a left-facing Bird Block, noting the direction of the units when piecing the block. Trim to 18½" (47cm) square.

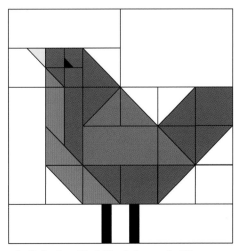

Left-Facing Bird Block Assembly Diagram

Nest Block

Block size: 18½" (47cm) square (Make 2)
Make one right-facing and one left-facing Nest Block. Refer to the Nest Block Assembly Diagrams throughout assembly. Stich and press as desired, taking care to nest the seams by pressing in alternating directions. Note: Seams that don't need nesting can be pressed in either direction. Trim to 18½" (47cm) square.

UNIT ASSEMBLY

1. Following the Corner Flip instructions on page 10, make the following CF units, pressing the seams open.

- (4) 3½" x 6½" (8.9cm x 16.5cm) White/Orange CF units from (4) 3½" x 6½" (8.9cm x 16.5cm) White horizontal rectangles and (4) 1¼" (3.2cm) Orange squares, sewing an orange square on the bottom right corner of two rectangles and the bottom left corner of the remaining rectangles

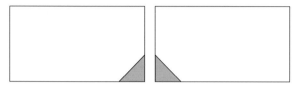

Make 2 of Each

- (2) 1¼" x 2" (3.2cm x 5.1cm) Yellow/Orange CF units from (2) 1¼" x 2" (3.2cm x 5.1cm) Yellow horizontal rectangles and (2) 1¼" (3.2cm) Orange squares, sewing an orange square on the upper right corner of one rectangle and the upper left corner of the remaining rectangle

Make 1 of Each

- (2) 2" x 2¾" (5.1cm x 7cm) Yellow/Black/White CF units from (2) 2" x 2¾" (5.1cm x 7cm) Yellow vertical rectangles, (2) 1¼" (3.2cm) Black squares, and (2) 1¼" (3.2cm) White squares, sewing the black squares in the upper right corner of (1) Yellow rectangle and upper left corner of remaining Yellow rectangle and the White squares in the opposite corners as shown

Make 1 of Each

- (4) 2" x 3½" (8.9cm) Yellow/White CF units from (4) 2" x 3½" (8.9cm) Yellow horizontal rectangles and (8) 1¼" (3.2cm) White squares, sewing a white background square in the upper left and right corners of each yellow rectangle

Make 4

- (2) 3½" (8.9cm) Turquoise/White CF units and (4) 3½" (8.9cm) Aqua/White CF units from (2) 3½" (8.9cm) Turquoise squares, (4) 3½" (8.9cm) Aqua squares, and (12) 1¼" (3.2cm) White squares, sewing white background squares on the upper left and right corners of each Aqua and Turquoise square

Make 2   Make 4

- (4) 2" (5.1cm) Turquoise/Yellow CF units from (4) 2" (5.1cm) Turquoise squares and (8) 1¼" (3.2cm) Yellow squares, sewing a yellow square on the upper right and left corners of each Turquoise square. (Note: Sew and corner flip the yellow squares, one at a time; it doesn't matter which one gets sewn and corner flipped first, they are supposed to overlap.)

Make 4

- (2) 8" x 12½" (20.3cm x 31.8cm) Tan/White CF units from (2) 8" x 12½" (20.3cm x 31.8cm) Tan horizontal rectangles and (4) 3½" (8.9cm) White squares, sewing the White squares onto the bottom left and right corners of the Tan rectangle

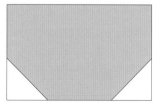

Make 2

NEST BLOCK ASSEMBLY

Each block uses:

- (2) 3½" (8.9cm) Aqua/White CF units
- (1) 3½" (8.9cm) Turquoise/White CF unit
- (2) 2" (5.1cm) Turquoise/Yellow CF units
- (2) 2" x 3½" (5.1cm x 8.9cm) Yellow/White CF units
- (1) 2" x 2¾" (5.1cm x 7cm) Yellow/Black/White CF unit
- (1) 1¼" x 2" (3.2cm x 5.1cm) Yellow/Orange CF unit
- (2) 3½" x 6½" (8.9cm x 16.5cm) White/Orange CF units
- (1) 8" x 12½" (20.3cm x 31.8cm) Tan/White CF unit
- (1) 2" x 12½" (5.1cm x 31.8cm) White rectangle
- (1) 3½" x 6½" (8.9cm x 16.5cm) White rectangle
- (2) 3½" x 18½" (8.9cm x 47cm) White rectangles
- (1) 3½" White square

2. Referring to the Nest Block Assembly Diagram, join the units in rows as follows:

Row 1: Join (1) 3½" x 6½" (8.9cm x 16.5cm) White/Orange CF unit and (1) 3½" x 6½" (8.9cm x 16.5cm) White rectangle

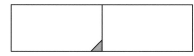

Row 2: Join (1) 2" x 2¾" (5.1cm x 7cm) Yellow/Black/White CF unit and (1) 1¼" x 2" (3.2cm x 5.1cm) Yellow/Orange CF unit as shown. Sew (1) 2" x 3½" (5.1cm x 8.9cm) Yellow/White CF unit to the left side of the eye/beak unit. Sew (1) 3½" (8.9cm) White square to the left side of the unit and (1) 3½" x 6½" (8.9cm x 16.5cm) White/Orange CF unit to the right (orange corners facing).

Row 3: Join (2) 2" (5.1cm) Turquoise/Yellow CF units, then sew (1) 2" x 3½" (5.1cm x 8.9cm) Yellow/White CF unit to the top of the unit. Sew (1) 3½" (8.9cm) Aqua/White CF to either side of the Turquoise/Yellow CF unit, then sew (1) 3½" (8.9cm) Turquoise unit to the right side. Join (1) 8" x 12½" (20.3cm x 31.8cm) Tan/White CF unit and (1) 2" x 12½" (5.1cm x 31.8cm) White rectangle to the bottom as shown.

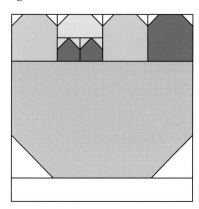

3. Join the rows. Sew (1) 3½" x 18½" (8.9cm x 47cm) White rectangle to either side of the unit to complete the Nest Block. In the same manner as above, make a left-facing Nest block noting the orientation of the units when piecing the block.

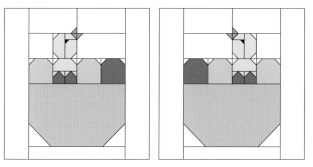

Left- and Right-Facing Nest Block
Assembly Diagrams

Finishing the Quilt

1. Referring to the Quilt Assembly Diagram, sew the blocks together in rows of 2. Join the rows.

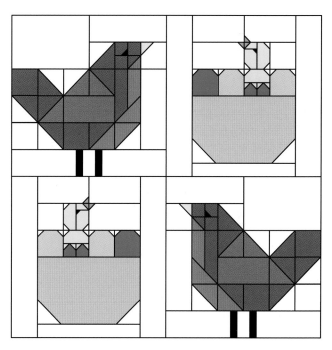

Quilt Assembly Diagram

2. Layer the quilt top, batting, and backing; baste. Quilt as desired.

3. Bind the quilt.

Spring Fling

Seeing the first hints of spring after a long, cold winter always make my heart sing! This generously sized throw is decorated with rows of colorful birds marching back and forth between starbursts of spring blossoms. This design calls for 15 bird blocks and 15 flower blocks joined in rows of five and framed with a narrow border. Layout the blocks as shown or create your own design.

64" x 76" (162.6 x 193cm)
Designed, pieced, and quilted by Sherilyn Mortensen
Fabric: Moda Grunge, Alison Glass, stash

Fabric Requirements

- ½ yard (0.5m) each Pink and Purple
- ⅓ yard (0.3m) each Light Pink, Medium Pink, and Teal
- ¼ yard (0.2m) each Peach, Blue, Aqua, Light Teal, Yellow, Light Yellow, Light Orange, and Light Green
- 6" (15cm) x width of fabric (WOF) each Light Peach, Plum, and Light Blue
- ⅛ yard (0.1m) Dark Teal and Dark Purple
- 15" (38.1m) x WOF Gold
- 20" (50.8cm) x WOF Orange
- ⅔ yard (0.6m) Green
- 7" (17.8cm) x WOF Dark Green
- 3" (7.6cm) x WOF Black
- 4½ yards (4.1m) White Background (BG)
- 4½ yards (4.1m) Backing
- 20" (50.8cm) x WOF Binding

Cutting Instructions

From Pink fabric (Pink Bird body and Medium Pink Flower center petals), cut:
- (11) 3½" (8.9cm) squares
- (15) 2½" (6.4cm) squares
- (3) 1½" x 2½" (3.8 x 6.4cm) rectangles
- (6) 2½" x 4½" (6.4cm x 11.4cm) rectangles
- (18) 1½" (3.8cm) squares

From Medium Pink fabric (Medium Pink Flower outside petals), cut:
- (24) 3½" (8.9cm) squares
- (12) 2½" (6.4cm) squares

From Light Pink fabric, cut (Medium Pink Flower middle petals):
- (12) 3½" (8.9cm) squares
- (12) 2½" (6.4cm) squares
- (12) 1½" (3.8cm) squares

From Plum fabric, cut: (Gold Flower center petals)
- (12) 2½" (6.4cm) squares
- (12) 1½" (3.8cm) squares

From Peach fabric, cut: (Peach Bird body)
- (11) 3½" (8.9cm) squares
- (6) 1½" (3.8cm) squares
- (3) 2½" (6.4cm) squares
- (3) 1½" x 2½" (3.8cm x 6.4cm) rectangles
- (6) 2½" x 4½" (6.4cm x 11.4cm) rectangles

From Light Peach fabric (Orange Flower center petals), cut:
- (12) 2½" (6.4cm) squares
- (12) 1½" (3.8cm) squares

From Blue fabric (Blue Bird body), cut:
- (11) 3½" (8.9cm) squares
- (6) 1½" (3.8cm) squares
- (3) 2½" (6.4cm) squares
- (3) 1½" x 2½" (3.8cm x 6.4cm) rectangles
- (6) 2½" x 4½" (6.4cm x 11.4cm) rectangles

From Light Blue fabric (Blue Bird wing), cut:
- (5) 3½" (8.9cm) squares
- (3) 2½" x 4½" (6.4cm x 11.4cm) rectangles

From Aqua fabric (Purple Flower middle petals), cut:
- (12) 3½" (8.9cm) squares
- (12) 2½" (6.4cm) squares
- (12) 1½" (3.8cm) squares

From Teal fabric (Teal Flower outside petals), cut:
- (24) 3½" (8.9cm) squares
- (12) 2½" (6.4cm) squares

From Dark Teal fabric (Teal Flower center petals), cut:
- (12) 2½" (6.4cm) squares
- (12) 1½" (3.8cm) squares

From Light Teal fabric (Teal Flower middle petals), cut:
- (12) 3½" (8.9cm) squares
- (12) 2½" (6.4cm) squares
- (12) 1½" (3.8cm) squares

From Purple fabric (Purple Flower outside petals, Pink Bird wing), cut:
- (29) 3½" (8.9cm) squares
- (3) 2½" x 4½" (6.4cm x 11.4cm) rectangles
- (12) 2½" (6.4cm) squares

From Dark Purple fabric (Purple Flowers center petals), cut:
- (12) 2½" (6.4cm) squares
- (12) 1½" (3.8cm) squares

From Yellow fabric (Yellow Bird body), cut:
- (11) 3½" (8.9cm) squares
- (6) 1½" (3.8cm) squares
- (3) 2½" (6.4cm) squares
- (3) 1½" x 2½" (3.8cm x 6.4cm) rectangles
- (6) 2½" x 4½" (6.4cm x 11.4cm) rectangles

From Light Yellow fabric (Gold Flower middle petals), cut:
- (12) 3½" (8.9cm) squares
- (12) 2½" (6.4cm) squares
- (12) 1½" (3.8cm) squares

From Gold fabric (Gold Flower outside petals and 12 beaks), cut:
- (24) 3½" (8.9cm) squares
- (12) 2½" (6.4cm) squares
- (12) 1½" (3.8cm) squares

From Orange fabric (Orange Flower outside petals/ Yellow Bird wing/Peach Bird wing and 3 beaks), cut:
- (34) 3½" (8.9cm) squares
- (12) 2½" (6.4cm) squares
- (6) 2½" x 4½" (6.4cm x 11.4cm) rectangles
- (3) 1½" (3.8cm) squares

From Light Orange fabric (Orange Flower middle petals), cut:
- (12) 3½" (8.9cm) squares
- (12) 2½" (6.4cm) squares
- (12) 1½" (3.8cm) squares

From Dark Green fabric (Light Green Bird wing), cut:
- (5) 3½" (8.9cm) squares
- (3) 2½" x 4½" (6.4cm x 11.4cm) rectangles

From Green fabric (leaves), cut:
- (60) 3½" (8.9cm) squares

From Light Green fabric (Light Green Bird body), cut:
- (11) 3½" (8.9cm) squares
- (6) 1½" (3.8cm) squares
- (3) 2½" (6.4cm) squares
- (3) 1½" x 2½" (3.8cm x 6.4cm) rectangles
- (6) 2½" x 4½" (6.4cm x 11.4cm) rectangles

From Black fabric (bird legs/eyes), cut:
- (30) 1" x 2½" (2.5cm x 6.4cm) rectangles
- (15) 1" (2.5cm) squares

From White background fabric, cut:
- (169) 3½" (8.9cm) squares
- (90) 2½" (6.4cm) squares
- (30) 2½" x 5½" (6.4cm x 14cm) rectangles
- (30) 2½" x 6½" (6.4cm x 16.5cm) rectangles
- (15) 4½" x 6½" (11.4cm x 16.5cm) rectangles
- (15) 1½" x 2½" (3.8cm x 6.4cm) rectangles
- (8) 2½" (6.4cm) x width of fabric (WOF) (borders), selvedge edges trimmed

Assembly

1. Following the Half Square Triangle (HST) directions on page 8, make the following HST units from 3½" (8.9cm) squares. Press seams open and trim to 2½" (6.4cm) square. Note: Some of HST units will not be used.

- (15) Pink/White units from (8) squares each (Pink birds)
Make 15
- (6) Pink/Purple units from (3) squares each (Pink Birds)
Make 6
- (15) Peach/White units from (8) squares each (Peach Birds)
Make 15
- (6) Peach/Orange units from (3) squares each (Peach Birds)
Make 6
- (15) Blue/White units from (8) squares each (Blue Birds)
Make 15
- (6) Blue/Light Blue units from (3) squares each (Blue Birds)
Make 6
- (3) Light Blue/White units from (2) squares each (Blue Birds)
Make 3
- (15) Yellow/White units from (8) square each (Yellow Birds)
Make 15
- (6) Yellow/Orange units from (3) squares each (Yellow Birds)
Make 6
- (15) Light Green/White units from (8) squares each (Light Green Birds)
Make 15
- (3) Dark Green/White units from (2) squares each (Light Green Birds)
Make 3
- (6) Light Green/Dark Green units from (3) squares each (Light Green Birds)
Make 6
- (27) Purple/White units from (14) squares each (Pink Birds, Purple Flowers)
Make 27
- (30) Orange/White units from (15) squares each (Peach Birds, Yellow Birds, Orange Flowers)
Make 30

- (24) Gold/White units from (12) squares each (Gold Flowers)
Make 24
- (24) Medium Pink/White units from (12) squares each (Medium Pink Flowers)
Make 24
- (24) Teal/White units from (12) squares each (Teal Flowers)
Make 24
- (24) Gold/Light Yellow units from (12) squares each (Gold Flowers)
Make 24
- (24) Medium Pink/Light Pink units from (12) squares each (Medium Pink Flowers)
Make 24
- (24) Purple/Aqua units from (12) squares each (Purple Flowers)
Make 24
- (24) Teal/Light Teal units from (12) squares each (Teal Flowers)
Make 24
- (24) Orange/Light Orange units from (12) squares each (Orange flowers)
Make 24
- (120) Green/White units from (60) squares each (Leaves)
Make 120

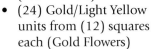
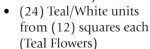

2. Make the following HST units from 2½" (6.4cm) squares. Press the seams open and trim to 1½" (3.8cm) square.

- (24) Light Yellow/Plum units from (12) squares each
- (24) Light Pink/Pink units from (12) squares each
Make 24
- (24) Aqua/Dark Purple units from (12) squares each
Make 24
- (24) Light Orange/Light Peach units from (12) squares each
Make 24
- (24) Light Teal/Dark Teal units from (12) squares each
Make 24

3. Following the Corner Flip (CF) instructions on page 10, make (12) 2½" (6.4cm) White/Gold CF units for beaks, sewing (1) 1½" (3.8cm) Gold square onto a corner of (1) 2½" (6.4cm) White square.

In the same manner, make (3) 2½" (6.4cm) White/Orange CF units for beaks using (3) 2½" (6.4cm) White and (3) 1½" (3.8cm) Orange squares, sewing (1) orange square on a corner of each White square.

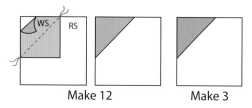

Make 12   Make 3

4. Make (3) 1½" (3.8cm) Pink/Black CF units for eyes, sewing (1) 1" (2.5cm) Black square onto the corner of each 1½" (3.8cm) Pink square. In the same manner, make (3) 1½" (3.8cm) CF units each in Peach/Black, Blue/Black, Yellow/Black, and Light Green/Black.

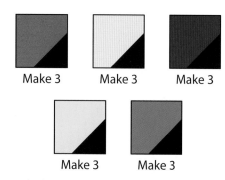

Make 3   Make 3   Make 3

Make 3   Make 3

Bird Block Assembly

Block size: 12½" (31.8cm) square
All of the right- and left-facing blocks are constructed in the same manner; refer to the Block Assembly Diagrams for placement and orientation of HST and CF units. Press seams, taking care to alternate pressing directions to nest the seams. Seams that don't need nesting can be pressed in either direction. Make (2) right-facing and (1) left-facing Bird Block each in Pink, Peach, Yellow, Blue, and Light Green.

Assemble (1) Pink Bird Block using:
- (5) 2½" (6.4cm) Pink/White HST units
- (1) 2½" (6.4cm) Purple/White HST unit
- (2) 2½" (6.4cm) Pink/Purple HST units
- (1) 2½" x 4½" (6.4cm x 11.4cm) Purple rectangle
- (1) 2½" (6.4cm) Pink square
- (2) 2½" x 4½" (6.4cm x 11.4cm) Pink rectangles
- (1) 1½" (3.8cm) Pink square
- (1) 1½" x 2½" (3.8cm x 6.4cm) Pink rectangle
- (2) 1" x 2½" (2.5cm x 6.4cm) Black rectangles
- (1) 1½" (3.8cm) Pink/Black CF unit
- (1) 2½" (6.4cm) White/Gold CF unit
- (1) 2½" (6.4cm) White square
- (1) 1½" x 2½" (3.8cm x 6.4cm) White rectangle
- (2) 2½" x 5½" (6.4cm x 14cm) White rectangles
- (2) 2½" x 6½" (6.4cm x 16.5cm) White rectangles
- (1) 4½" x 6½" (11.4cm x 16.5cm) White rectangle

1. Referring to the diagram, make the head section. Join (1) 1½" (3.8cm) Pink/Black CF unit and (1) 1½" (3.8cm) Pink square. Sew (1) 2½" (6.4cm) Pink/White HST unit to the left side and (1) 1½" x 2½" (3.8cm x 6.4cm) Pink vertical rectangle to the right. Join (1) 2½" (6.4cm) White/Gold CF unit to the right side of the Pink rectangle. In this order, sew (1) 2½" x 6½" (6.4cm x 16.5cm) White rectangle to the top of the unit and sew (1) 4½" x 6½" (11.4cm x 16.5cm) White rectangle to the left side.

2. Referring to the diagram for placement and orientation, join the following units in sections, then join the sections.
Tail Section: Join (1) 2½" (6.4cm) Pink square, (3) 2½" (6.4cm) Pink/White HST units, (1) 2½" (6.4cm) Pink/Purple HST unit, and (1) 2½" (6.4cm) White square as shown.
Body Section: Referring to the diagram, join (1) 2½" (6.4cm) square HST unit each in Purple/White and Pink/Purple. Join (1) 2½" x 4½" (6.4cm x 11.4cm) rectangle each in Pink and Purple as shown.

Chest Section: Join (1) 2½" x 4½" (6.4cm x 11.4cm) Pink rectangle and (1) 2½" (6.4cm) Pink/White HST unit. Sew (1) 2½" x 6½" (6.4cm x 16.5cm) White rectangle along the right side.

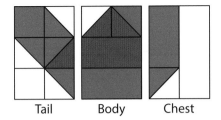

Tail   Body   Chest

3. Join (2) 2½" x 5½" (6.4cm x 14cm) White rectangles, (2) 1" x 2½" (2.5cm x 6.4cm) Black rectangles, and (1) 1½" x 2½" (3.8cm x 6.4cm) White rectangle, alternating the placement of the units as shown.

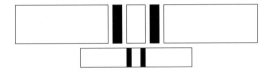

4. Join the rows to form the block. Make (2) right-facing Bird Blocks.

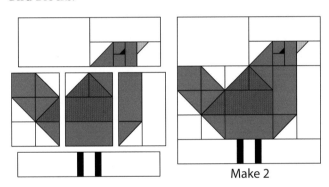

Make 2

Right-Facing Bird Block Assembly Diagram

5. Referring to the left-facing Bird Block Diagram for placement and orientation of the units, make (1) left-facing Pink Bird Block.

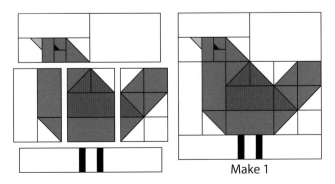

Make 1

Left-Facing Bird Block Assembly Diagram

7. Following the Pink Bird Block directions, make (2) right-facing and (1) left-facing Bird Blocks each in Peach, Yellow, Blue, and Light Green.

For each Peach Bird Block, you will need:

- (5) 2½" (6.4cm) Peach/White HST units
- (1) 2½" (6.4cm) Orange/White HST unit
- (2) 2½" (6.4cm) Peach/Orange HST units
- (1) 2½" x 4½" (6.4cm x 11.4cm) Orange rectangle
- (1) 2½" (6.4cm) Peach square
- (2) 2½" x 4½" (6.4cm x 11.4cm) Peach rectangles
- (1) 1½" (3.8cm) Peach square
- (1) 1½" x 2½" (3.8cm x 6.4cm) Peach rectangle
- (2) 1" x 2½" (2.5cm x 6.4cm) Black rectangles
- (1) 1½" (3.8cm) Peach/Black CF unit
- (1) 2½" (6.4cm) White/Gold CF unit
- (1) 2½" (6.4cm) White square
- (1) 1½" x 2½" (3.8cm x 6.4cm) White rectangle
- (2) 2½" x 5½" (6.4cm x 14cm) White rectangles
- (2) 2½" x 6½" (6.4cm x 16.5cm) White rectangles
- (1) 4½" x 6½" (11.4cm x 16.5cm) White rectangle

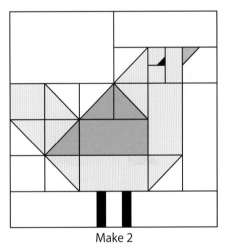

Make 2

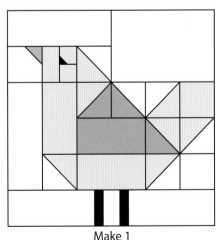

Make 1

For each Blue Bird Block, you will need:
- (5) 2½" (6.4cm) Blue/White HST units
- (1) 2½" (6.4cm) Light Blue/White HST unit
- (2) 2½" (6.4cm) Blue/Light Blue HST units
- (1) 2½" x 4½" (6.4cm x 11.4cm) Light Blue rectangle
- (1) 2½" (6.4cm) Blue square
- (2) 2½" x 4½" (6.4cm x 11.4cm) Blue rectangles
- (1) 1½" (3.8cm) Blue square
- (1) 1½" x 2½" (3.8cm x 6.4cm) Blue rectangle
- (2) 1" x 2½" (2.5cm x 6.4cm) Black rectangles
- (1) 1½" (3.8cm) Blue/Black CF unit
- (1) 2½" (6.4cm) White/Gold CF unit
- (1) 2½" (6.4cm) White square
- (1) 1½" x 2½" (3.8cm x 6.4cm) White rectangle
- (2) 2½" x 5½" (6.4cm x 14cm) White rectangles
- (2) 2½" x 6½" (6.4cm x 16.5cm) White rectangles
- (1) 4½" x 6½" (11.4cm x 16.5cm) White rectangle

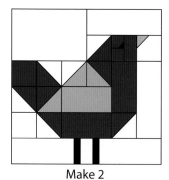

Make 2

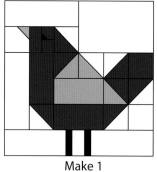

Make 1

For each Yellow Bird Block, you will need:
- (5) 2½" (6.4cm) Yellow/White HST units
- (1) 2½" (6.4cm) Orange/White HST unit
- (2) 2½" (6.4cm) Yellow/Orange HST units
- (1) 2½" x 4½" (6.4cm x 11.4cm) Orange rectangle
- (1) 2½" (6.4cm) Yellow square
- (2) 2½" x 4½" (6.4cm x 11.4cm) Yellow rectangles
- (1) 1½" (3.8cm) Yellow square
- (1) 1½" x 2½" (3.8cm x 6.4cm) Yellow rectangle
- (2) 1" x 2½" (2.5cm x 6.4cm) Black rectangles
- (1) 1½" (3.8cm) Yellow/Black CF unit
- (1) 2½" (6.4cm) White/Orange CF unit
- (1) 2½" (6.4cm) White square
- (1) 1½" x 2½" (3.8cm x 6.4cm) White rectangle
- (2) 2½" x 5½" (6.4cm x 14cm) White rectangles
- (2) 2½" x 6½" (6.4cm x 16.5cm) White rectangles
- (1) 4½" x 6½" (11.4cm x 16.5cm) White rectangle

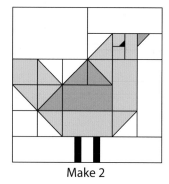

Make 2

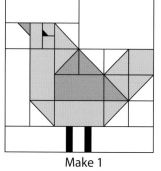

Make 1

For each Light Green Bird Block, you will need:
- (5) 2½" (6.4cm) Light Green/White HST units
- (1) 2½" (6.4cm) Dark Green/White HST unit
- (2) 2½" (6.4cm) Light Green/Dark Green HST units
- (1) 2½" x 4½" (6.4cm x 11.4cm) Dark Green rectangle
- (1) 2½" (6.4cm) Light Green square
- (2) 2½" x 4½" (6.4cm x 11.4cm) Light Green rectangles
- (1) 1½" (3.8cm) Light Green square
- (1) 1½" x 2½" (3.8cm x 6.4cm) Light Green rectangle
- (2) 1" x 2½" (2.5cm x 6.4cm) Black rectangles
- (1) 1½" (3.8cm) Light Green/Black CF unit
- (1) 2½" (6.4cm) White/Gold CF unit
- (1) 2½" (6.4cm) White square
- (1) 1½" x 2½" (3.8cm x 6.4cm) White rectangle
- (2) 2½" x 5½" (6.4cm x 14cm) White rectangles
- (2) 2½" x 6½" (6.4cm x 16.5cm) White rectangles
- (1) 4½" x 6½" (11.4cm x 16.5cm) White rectangle

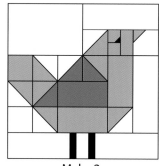

Make 2

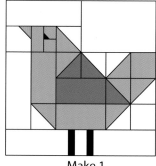

Make 1

Flower Block Assembly

Block size: 12½" (31.8cm) square
All flower blocks are assembled in the same manner. Refer to the Flower Block Assembly Diagram for placement and orientation of units. Stitch and press as desired. Make (3) Flower blocks each in Medium Pink, Purple, Orange, Teal, and Gold.

For each Medium Pink Flower Block, you will need:
- (8) 2½" (6.4cm) Green/White HST units
- (8) 2½" (6.4cm) Medium Pink/White HST units
- (8) 2½" (6.4cm) Medium Pink/Light Pink HST units
- (8) 1½" (3.8cm) Light Pink/Pink HST units
- (4) 2½" (6.4cm) White squares
- (4) 2½" (6.4cm) Medium Pink squares
- (4) 1½" (3.8cm) Light Pink squares
- (4) 1½" (3.8cm) Pink squares

1. Join (2) 1½" (3.8cm) Light Pink/Pink HST units, (1) 1½" (3.8cm) Light Pink square, and (1) 1½" (3.8cm) Pink square in a four patch as shown. Make 4 units.

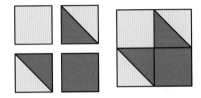

2. Join the following 2½" (6.4cm) units in rows:
Row 1: (1) White square, (1) Green/White HST unit, (1) Medium Pink/White HST unit
Row 2: (1) Green/White HST unit, (1) Medium Pink square, (1) Medium Pink/Light Pink HST unit
Row 3: (1) Medium Pink/White HST unit, (1) Medium Pink/Light Pink HST unit, (1) Pink/Light Pink double HST unit
Join the rows together. Make 4 units.

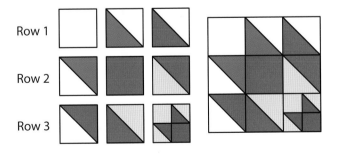

3. Sew the units together in rows of 2. Join the rows, pressing the center seams open. Make (3) Flower blocks in Medium Pink.

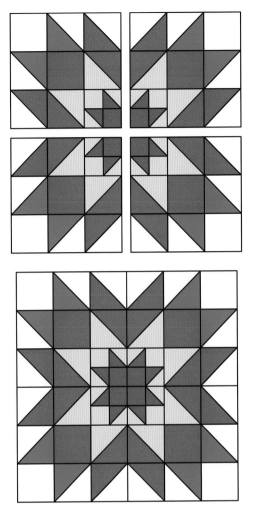

Flower Block Assembly Diagram
(Make 3)

4. In the same manner, make 3 Flower blocks each in Gold, Purple, Orange, and Teal.

For each Gold Flower block, you will need:
- (8) 2½" (6.4cm) Green/White HST units
- (8) 2½" (6.4cm) Gold/White HST units
- (8) 2½" (6.4cm) Gold/Light Yellow HST units
- (8) 1½" (3.8cm) Light Yellow/Plum HST units
- (4) 2½" (6.4cm) White squares
- (4) 2½" (6.4cm) Gold squares
- (4) 1½" (3.8cm) Light Yellow squares
- (4) 1½" (3.8cm) Plum squares

Make 3

For each Purple Flower block, you will need:
- (8) 2½" (6.4cm) Green/White HST units
- (8) 2½" (6.4cm) Purple/White HST units
- (8) 2½" (6.4cm) Purple/Aqua HST units
- (8) 1½" (3.8cm) Aqua/Dark Purple HST units
- (4) 2½" (6.4cm) White squares
- (4) 2½" (6.4cm) Purple squares
- (4) 1½" (3.8cm) Aqua squares
- (4) 1½" (3.8cm) Dark Purple squares

Make 3

For each Orange Flower block, you will need:
- (8) 2½" (6.4cm) Green/White HST units
- (8) 2½" (6.4cm) Orange/White HST units
- (8) 2½" (6.4cm) Orange/Light Orange HST units
- (8) 1½" (3.8cm) Light Orange/Light Peach HST units
- (4) 2½" (6.4cm) White squares
- (4) 2½" (6.4cm) Orange squares
- (4) 1½" (3.8cm) Light Orange squares
- (4) 1½" (3.8cm) Light Peach squares

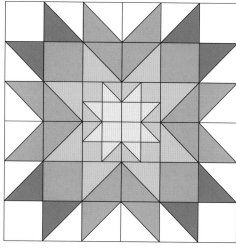

Make 3

Assemble (1) Teal flower using the following pieces:
- (8) 2½" (6.4cm) Green/White HST units
- (8) 2½" (6.4cm) Teal/White HST units
- (8) 2½" (6.4cm) Teal/Light Teal HST units
- (8) 1½" (3.8cm) Light Teal/Dark Teal HST units
- (4) 2½" (6.4cm) White squares
- (4) 2½" (6.4cm) Teal squares
- (4) 1½" (3.8cm) Light Teal squares
- (4) 1½" (3.8cm) Dark Teal squares

Make 3

Finishing the Quilt Top

1. Referring to the Quilt Assembly Diagram, join the blocks in rows of (5) as shown.

2. Join (2) 2½" (6.4cm) x WOF White border strips end to end and press. Make (4) border strips total.

3. Sew a border strip to either side of the quilt top. Trim to fit and press. Sew a border strip to the top and bottom of the quilt top. Trim and press.

4. Layer the backing, batting, and quilt top; baste. Quilt as desired.

5. Bind the quilt.

Quilt Top Assembly Diagram

Daisy Chain

Daisies are one of my favorite flowers. Their classic, elegant blooms are just right for almost any occasion. They add an eye-catching design element to this five-block quilt, which makes a perfect table runner or wall hanging.

Finished Size: 16" x 64" (40.6cm x 162.6cm)
Designed, pieced, and quilted by Sherilyn Mortensen
Quilt bound by Amy Maxfield
Fabrics: Kaufman Essex, Valorie Wells, plus stash

Fabric Requirements

- ¼ yard (0.2m) each Dark Yellow, Medium Yellow, and Light Yellow
- 4" (10.2cm) x Width of Fabric (WOF) or (1) 12" (30.5cm) square Yellow
- ½ yard (0.5m) White
- 6" (15.2cm) x WOF each Green and Light Green
- 1 yard (0.9m) Dark Gray Background fabric
- 2¾ yard (2.5m) Backing fabric
- ⅓ yard (0.3m) Binding fabric

Cutting Instructions

From Dark Yellow fabric, cut:
- (2) 4" (10.2cm) squares
- (6) 3½" (8.9cm) squares

From Medium Yellow fabric, cut:
- (2) 4" (10.2cm) squares
- (6) 3½" (8.9cm) squares

From Light Yellow fabric, cut:
- (2) 4" (10.2cm) squares
- (6) 3½" (8.9cm) squares

From Yellow fabric, cut:
- (6) 3½" (8.9cm) squares

From White fabric, cut:
- (6) 4" (10.2cm) squares
- (24) 3½" (8.9cm) squares
- (12) 2½" (6.4cm) squares

From Green fabric, cut:
- (8) 3½" (8.9cm) squares
- (4) 1½" x 6½" (3.8cm x 16.5cm)

From Light Green fabric, cut:
- (8) 3½" (8.9cm) squares
- (4) 1½" x 6½" (3.8cm x 16.5cm) rectangles

From Dark Gray Background fabric, cut:
- (40) 3½" (8.9cm) squares
- (12) 2½" (6.4cm) squares
- (8) 2½" x 4½" (6.4cm x 11.4cm) rectangles
- (4) 1½" x 12½" (3.8cm x 31.8cm) strips
- (4) 2½" x width-of-fabric (WOF) strips (trim the selvedge edges)

Assembly

1. Following the Half Square Triangle (HST) directions on page 8, make the following HST units from 3½" (8.9cm) squares. Press seams open and trim each unit to 2½" (6.4cm) square.
- (48) White/Dark Gray BG units from (24) squares each
- (4) Dark Yellow/Yellow units from (2) squares each
- (4) Light Yellow/Yellow units from (2) squares each
- (4) Medium Yellow/Yellow units from (2) squares each

Make 48   Make 4 of Each

2. Make the following HST units from 4" (10.2cm) squares, pressing seams open. Do not square. These units will be used for the Quarter Half Square Triangles (QHST) in step 3.
- (4) White/Dark Yellow units from (2) squares each
- (4) White/Medium Yellow units from (2) squares each
- (4) White/Light Yellow units from (2) squares each

Make 4 of Each

3. Following the Quarter Half Square Triangle (QHST) instructions on page 9, make the following QHST units. Press the seams open and trim each unit to 2½" (6.4cm) square.

- (8) White/Dark Yellow/Dark Yellow units from (4) 3½" (8.9cm) White/Dark Yellow HST units (not squared) and (4) 3½" (8.9cm) Dark Yellow squares
- (8) White/Medium Yellow/Medium Yellow units from (4) 3½" (8.9cm) White/Medium Yellow HST units (not squared) and (4) 3½" (8.9cm) Medium Yellow squares
- (8) White/Light Yellow/Light Yellow units from (4) 3½" (8.9cm) White/Light Yellow HST units (not squared) and (4) 3½" (8.9cm) Light Yellow squares

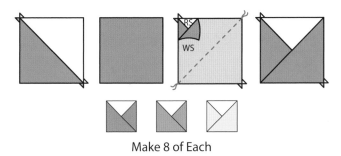

Make 8 of Each

Daisy Block Assembly

Block size: 12½" (31.8cm) square (make 3 blocks total)

Assemble (1) Dark Yellow Daisy block using:
- (16) 2½" (3.8cm) White/Dark Gray BG HST units
- (8) 2½" (3.8cm) White/Dark Yellow/Dark Yellow QHST units
- (4) 2½" (3.8cm) Dark Yellow/Yellow HST units
- (4) 2½" (3.8cm) White Squares
- (4) 2½" (3.8cm) Dark Gray BG squares

1. Referring to the diagram for placement and orientation, join the following units in rows:
Row 1: (1) 2½" (6.4cm) Dark Gray BG square and (2) 2½" (6.4cm) White/Dark Gray BG HST units

Row 2: (1) 2½" (6.4cm) White/Dark Gray BG HST unit, (1) 2½" (6.4cm) White square, and (1) 2½" (6.4cm) White/Dark Yellow/Dark Yellow QHST unit

Row 3: (1) 2½" (6.4cm) White/Dark Gray BG HST unit, (1) 2½" (6.4cm) White/Dark Yellow/Dark Yellow QHST unit, and (1) 2½" (6.4cm) Dark Yellow/Yellow HST unit. Sew the units together in rows of three.

Join the rows. Press the seams, alternating the pressing direction to nest the seams. Make 4 units.

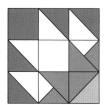

Make 4

2. Sew the units together in rows, then join the rows.

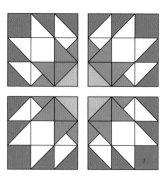 

Dark Yellow Daisy Block
(Make 1)

3. In the same manner, make (1) Daisy Block each in Medium Yellow and Light Yellow.

Assemble (1) Medium Yellow Daisy Block using:
- (16) 2½" (6.4cm) White/Dark Gray BG HST units
- (8) 2½" (6.4cm) White/Medium Yellow/Medium Yellow QHST units
- (4) 2½" (6.4cm) Medium Yellow/ Yellow HST units
- (4) 2½" (6.4cm) White Squares
- (4) 2½" (6.4cm) Dark Gray BG squares

Medium Yellow Daisy Block
(Make 1)

Assemble (1) Light Yellow Daisy Block using:
- (16) 2½" (6.4cm) White/Dark Gray BG HST units
- (8) 2½" (6.4cm) White/Light Yellow/ Light Yellow QHST units
- (4) 2½" (6.4cm) Light Yellow/Yellow HST units
- (4) 2½" (6.4cm) White Squares
- (4) 2½" (6.4cm) Dark Gray BG squares

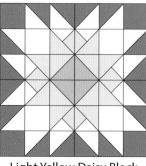

Light Yellow Daisy Block
(Make 1)

Leaf Block Assembly

Block size: 12½" (31.8cm) square (Make 2)

For each block, you will need:
- (8) 2½" (6.4cm) Green/Dark Gray BG HST units
- (8) 2½" (6.4cm) Light Green/Dark Gray BG HST units
- (2) 1½" x 6½" (3.8cm x 16.5cm) Green rectangles
- (2) 1½" x 6½" (3.8cm x 16.5cm) Light Green rectangles
- (4) 2½" x 4½" (6.4cm x 11.4cm) Dark Gray BG rectangles
- (2) 1½" x 12½" (3.8cm x 31.8cm) Dark Gray BG strips

1. Following the Half Square Triangle (HST) directions on page 8, make the following 2½" (6.4cm) units from 3½" (8.9cm) squares. Press and trim each unit to 2½" (6.4cm) square.
- (16) Green/Dark Gray BG units from (8) squares each
- (16) Light Green/Dark Gray BG units from (8) squares each

Make 16 of Each

2. Arrange (2) 2½" (6.4cm) Green/Dark Gray BG HST units and (2) 2½" (6.4cm) Light Green/Dark Gray BG HST units as shown. Sew the units together in rows, then join the rows. Press the seams, alternating the pressing direction to nest the seams. Seams that don't need nesting can be pressed in either direction. Make 4 units.

 Row 1
 Row 2

Make 4

3. Sew (1) 2½" x 4½" (6.4cm x 11.4cm) Dark Gray BG rectangle to the top of (1) HST unit and the bottom of the other, noting the color placement of the HST units. Sew (1) 1½" x 6½" (3.8cm x 16.5cm) green rectangle to the right side of two of the units and (1) 1½" x 6½" (3.8cm x 16.5cm) light green rectangle to the left of the remaining two units. Press the center seams open.

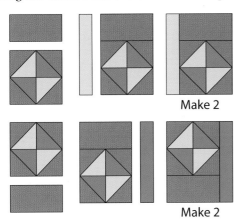

Make 2

Make 2

4. Join the units in rows as shown, then join the rows.

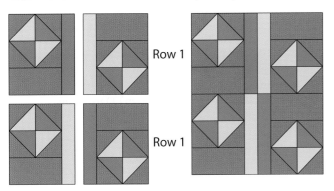

Row 1

Row 1

5. Sew (1) 1½" x 12½" (3.8cm x 31.8cm) Gray strip to either side of the block. Make 2 Leaf blocks.

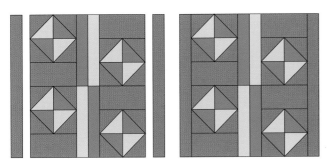

Finishing

1. Sew the blocks together as shown, alternating the designs.

2 . Cut (1) 2½" (6.4cm) x WOF gray border strip in half horizontally. Sew a half border strip to the end of a 2½" (6.4cm) x WOF gray border strip to make a long border strip. Press. Make (2) long gray borders. Join (1) side border to either side of the runner. Trim to fit and press.

3. Cut (1) 2½" (6.4cm) x WOF gray border strip in half horizontally. Sew one border strip to the top and bottom of the runner. Trim to fit and press.

Daisy Chain Assembly Diagram

4. Layer the quilt top, batting, and backing; baste. Quilt as desired.

5. Bind the quilt.

Heart to Heart

Whether you're getting through the last throes of winter or ushering in early spring, bright and cheery hearts are just the ticket to brighten your day! Twelve colorful, three-dimenional hearts make up this striking design, which is the perfect size for a baby quilt or a generous wall hanging.

Size: 36" x 48" (91.4cm x 121.9cm)
Designed, pieced, and quilted by Sherilyn Mortensen
Quilt bound by Amy Maxfield
Fabric: Moda Grunge, Tula Pink Assembly

Fabric Requirements
- 30" (76.2cm) x width of fabric (WOF) Purple
- 20" (50.8cm) x WOF Pink
- 15" (38.1cm) x WOF Peach
- 1 yard (0.9m) Gray
- 1 yard (0.9m) White
- 3 yards (2.7m) Backing fabric
- ⅓ yard (0.3m) Binding fabric

Cutting Instructions

From Purple fabric, cut:
- (6) 4½" (11.4cm) squares
- (3) 4" (10.2cm) squares
- (48) 3½" (8.9cm) squares
- (18) 2½" (6.4cm) squares

From Pink fabric, cut:
- (6) 4½" (11.4cm) squares
- (27) 3½" (8.9cm) squares
- (12) 2½" (6.4cm) squares

From Peach fabric, cut:
- (3) 4" (10.2cm) squares
- (21) 3½" (8.9cm) squares
- (6) 2½" (6.4cm) squares

From Gray fabric, cut:
- (3) 4" (10.2cm) squares
- (18) 3½" (8.9cm) squares
- (12) 2½" x 12½" (6.4cm x 31.8cm) rectangles
- (6) 2½" x 8½" (6.4cm x 21.6cm) rectangles
- (12) 2½" (6.4cm) squares

From White fabric, cut:
- (3) 4" (10.2cm) squares
- (18) 3½" (8.9cm) squares
- (12) 2½" x 12½" (6.4cm x 31.8cm) rectangles
- (6) 2½" x 8½" (6.4cm x 21.6cm) rectangles
- (12) 2½" (6.4cm) squares

Assembling the Units

1. Following the Half Square Triangle (HST) instructions on page 8, make the following HST units from 3½" (8.9cm) squares. Press the seams open and trim to 2½" (8.9cm) square.
- (24) Pink/Purple units from (12) squares each
- (24) Purple/Peach units from (12) squares each
- (18) Pink/White units from (9) squares each
- (18) Purple/White units from (9) squares each
- (18) Purple/Gray units from (9) squares each
- (18) Peach/Gray units from (9) squares each

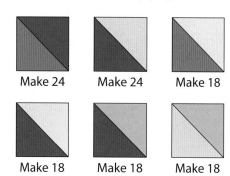

Make 24   Make 24   Make 18

Make 18   Make 18   Make 18

2. In the same manner, make the following HST units from 4" (10.2cm) squares. Do not square. These units will be used to make Quarter Half Square Triangles.
- (6) Purple/White units from (3) squares each
- (6) Peach/Gray units from (3) squares each

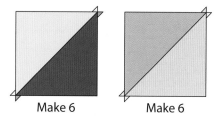

Make 6   Make 6

3. Following the Quarter Half Square Triangles (QHST) instructions on page 9, make the following QHST units. Press seams open and trim to 2½" (7.6cm) squares. Note: The remaining QHST units will not be used in this pattern.

- (6) Purple/White/Pink units (use the QHST unit as shown) from (6) 3½" (8.9cm) Purple/White HST units (not squared) and (6) 3½" (8.9cm) Pink squares

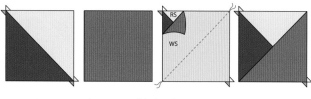

Make 6

- (6) Peach/Gray/Purple QHST units (use the QHST as shown) from (6) 3½" (8.9cm) Peach/Gray HST units (not squared) and (6) 3½" (8.9cm) Purple squares

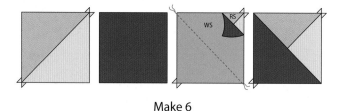

Make 6

Pink Heart Block Assembly

Block size: 12½" (31.8cm) (Make 6)
Refer to the Heart Block Assembly Diagram for steps 1–3 for placement and orientation of units. Press the seams as desired, taking care to nest the seams by alternating pressing directions. Seams that don't need nesting can be pressed in either direction.

Assemble (1) Pink Heart block using:
- (3) 2½" (6.4cm) Pink/White HST units
- (3) 2½" (6.4cm) Purple/White HST units
- (4) 2½" (6.4cm) Pink/Purple HST units
- (1) 2½" (6.4cm) Purple/White/Pink QHST unit
- (2) 2½" (6.4cm) Pink squares
- (1) 4½" (10.2cm) Pink square
- (1) 2½" (6.4cm) Purple square
- (2) 2½" (6.4cm) White squares
- (1) 2½" x 8½" (6.4cm x 21.6cm) White rectangle
- (2) 2½" x 12½" (6.4cm x 31.8cm) White rectangles

1. Join (1) 2½" (6.4cm) White square, (2) 2½" (6.4cm) Pink/White HST units, and (1) 2½" (6.4cm) Pink square as shown. Sew (1) 2½" x 8½" (6.4cm x 21.6cm) White rectangle to the left side of the unit to complete left section as shown.

2. Join (1) 2½" (6.4cm) Pink/Purple HST unit and (1) Purple/White/Pink QHST. Sew (1) 4½" (11.4cm) Pink square to the bottom of the unit. Join (1) Pink/White HST unit and (1) Pink/Purple HST unit, then sew the HST units to the bottom of the Pink square to complete center section as shown.

3. Referring to the diagram, join (1) 2½" (6.4cm) Purple/White HST unit, (2) 2½" (6.4cm) Purple/Pink HST units and (1) 2½" (6.4cm) Pink square in a column. Join (1) 2½" (6.4cm) White square, (2) 2½" (6.4cm) Purple/White HST units, and (1) 2½" (6.4cm) Purple square in a column. Sew the columns together as shown to complete right section as shown.

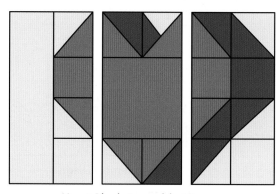

Heart Block Assembly Diagram

4. Join the sections as shown. Sew (1) 2½" x 12½" (6.4cm x 31.8cm) White rectangle to the top and bottom of the unit to complete the Heart Block. Make (6) blocks.

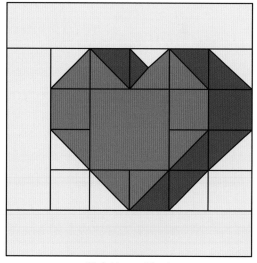

Pink Heart Block
(Make 6)

Purple Heart Block Assembly

Block size: 12½" (31.8cm) (Make 6)
Note: The Purple Heart Block has the opposite orientation of the Pink Heart Block.

In the same manner, assemble each Purple Heart block using:

- (3) 2½" (6.4cm) Purple/Gray HST units
- (3) 2½" (6.4cm) Peach/Gray HST units
- (4) 2½" (6.4cm) Purple/Peach HST units
- (1) 2½" (6.4cm) Peach/Gray/Purple QHST unit
- (2) 2½" (6.4cm) Purple squares
- (1) 4½" (10.2cm) Purple square
- (1) 2½" (6.4cm) Peach square
- (2) 2½" (6.4cm) Gray squares
- (1) 2½" x 8½" (6.4cm x 21.6cm) Gray rectangle
- (2) 2½" x 12½" (6.4cm x 31.8cm) Gray rectangles

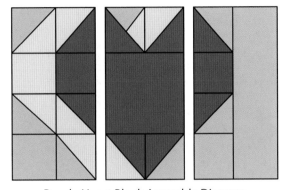

Purple Heart Block Assembly Diagram

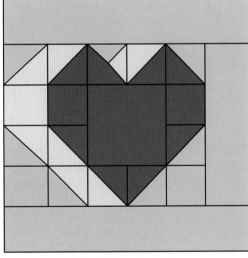

Purple Heart Block
(Make 6)

Finishing the Quilt Top

1. Join the blocks in rows of three, then join the rows and press.

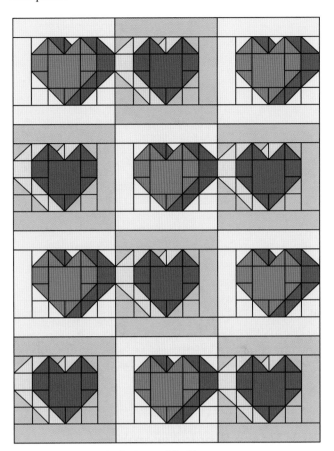

Quilt Assembly Diagram

2. Layer the quilt top, batting, and backing; baste. Quilt as desired.

3. Bind the quilt.

Juicy Fruit

Eye candy at its finest! These 12 delicious Juicy Fruit blocks make for a gorgeous and generously sized wall hanging or an adorable quilt. Cherries, watermelons, strawberries, and raspberries dressed in luscious reds and pinks will bring joy all summer long.

40" x 52" (101.6cm x 132.1cm)
Designed, pieced, and quilted by Sherilyn Mortensen
Quilt Bound by Amy Maxfield
Fabrics: Robin Pickens, Alison Glass, Moda Grunge, stash

Fabric Requirements

- 3" (7.6cm) x Width of Fabric (WOF) each Maroon, Light Maroon, and Bright White
- ⅓ yard (0.3m) each Red and Light Red
- ¼ yard (0.2m) each Purple, Light Purple, Pink, Green, Light Green, and Teal
- 6" (15.2cm) x WOF each Light Pink and Light Teal
- 2 yards (1.8m) White Background (BG) fabric
- 3 yards (2.7m) Backing fabric
- 15" (38.1) x WOF Binding fabric

Cutting Instructions:

From Maroon and Light Maroon fabric (cherries), cut:

- (12) 2½" (8.9cm) squares

From Red and Light Red fabric (strawberries), cut:

- (27) 2½" (8.9cm) squares
- (8) 3½" (8.9cm) squares

From Purple and Light Purple fabric (raspberries), cut:

- (15) 2½" (7.6cm) squares
- (3) 1½" x 2½" (3.8cm x 6.4cm) rectangles
- (5) 3½" (8.9cm) squares

From Pink fabric (watermelon), cut:

- (15) 2½" (7.6cm) squares
- (6) 1" (2.5cm) square
- (6) 1½" (3.8cm) square
- (6) 1½" x 6½" (3.8cm x 16.5cm) rectangles
- (3) 1½" x 8½" (3.8cm x 21.6cm) rectangles

From Light Pink fabric (watermelon), cut:

- (15) 2½" (6.4cm) squares
- (3) 1½" x 2½" (3.9cm x 6.4cm) rectangles

From Green fabric (watermelon), cut:

- (6) 1½"x 6½" (3.8cm x 16.5cm) rectangles
- (3) 1½" x 8½" (3.8cm x 21.6cm) rectangles
- (3) 3½" (8.9cm) squares

From Light Green fabric (cherries), cut:

- (3) 1½" x 4½" (3.8cm x 11.4cm) rectangles
- (6) 2½" (7.6cm) squares
- (6) 3½" (8.9cm) squares

From Teal fabric (strawberries), cut:

- (3) 1½" x 2½" (3.8cm x 6.4cm) rectangles
- (12) 3½" (8.9cm) squares

From Light Teal fabric (raspberries), cut:

- (3) 1" x 1½" (2.5cm x 3.8cm) rectangles
- (7) 3½" (8.9cm) squares

From Black fabric (watermelon seeds), cut:

- (36) 1" (2.5cm) squares

From Bright White fabric (strawberry/raspberry seeds):

- (111) 1" (2.5cm) squares

From White Background (BG) fabric, cut:

- (34) 3½" (8.9cm) squares
- (30) 1½" (3.8cm) squares
- (12) 2" (5.1cm) squares
- (9) 2½" x 12½" (6.4cm x 31.8cm) rectangles
- (3) 2½" x 3½" (6.4cm x 8.9cm) rectangles
- (6) 2½" x 6½" (6.4cm x 16.5cm) rectangles
- (12) 2½" (6.4cm) squares
- (12) 2" x 2½" (5.1cm x 6.4cm) rectangles
- (6) 2½" x 6" (6.4cm x 15.2cm) rectangles
- (6) 2½" x 10½" (6.4cm x 26.7cm) rectangles
- (3) 1½" x 8½" (3.8cm x 21.6cm) rectangles
- (6) 1½" x 2½" (3.8cm x 6.4cm) rectangles
- (6) 2½" x 4¼" (6.4cm x 11.4cm) rectangles
- (6) 2½" (6.4cm) x WOF border strips

Strawberry Block

Block size: 12½" (31.8cm) (Make 3)

UNIT ASSEMBLY

1. Following the HST instructions on page 8, make the following HST units from 3½" (8.9cm) squares. Press seams open and trim to 2½" (6.4cm) square. Note: Some units will not be used.

- (9) Red/White BG units from (5) squares each
- (9) Light Red/White BG units from (5) squares each
- (6) Red/Teal units from (3) squares each
- (6) Light Red/Teal units from (3) squares each
- (12) Teal/White BG units from (6) squares each

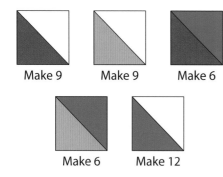

Make 9   Make 9   Make 6

Make 6   Make 12

2. Following the Corner Flip (CF) instructions on page 10, make the following CF units, pressing seams open.

- (18) Red/Bright White CF units from (18) 2½" (6.4cm) Red squares and (18) 1" (2.5cm) Bright White squares, joining a Bright White square onto one corner of each red square
- (9) Red/Bright White CF units from (9) 2½" (6.4cm) Red squares and (18) 1" (2.5cm) Bright White squares, joining (2) white squares onto opposite corners of each red square
- (24) Light Red/Bright White CF units from (24) 2½" (6.4cm) Light Red squares and (24) 1" (2.5cm) Bright White squares, joining a White square onto one corner of each Light Red square
- (3) Light Red/Bright White CF units from (3) 2½" (6.4cm) Light Red squares and (6) 1" (2.5cm) Bright White squares, joining (2) Bright White squares onto opposite corners of each Light Red square

Make 18   Make 9   Make 24   Make 3

BLOCK ASSEMBLY

Assemble (1) Strawberry block using:

- (9) 2½" (6.4cm) Red/Bright White CF units
- (9) 2½" (6.4cm) Light Red/Bright White CF units
- (3) 2½" (6.4cm) Red/BG HST units
- (3) 2½" (6.4cm) Light Red/BG HST units
- (2) 2½" (6.4cm) Red/Teal HST units
- (2) 2½" (6.4cm) Light Red/Teal HST units
- (4) 2½" (6.4cm) Teal/BG HST units
- (1) 1½" x 2½" (3.8cm x 6.4cm) Teal rectangle
- (2) 2" x 2½" (5.1cm x 6.4cm) White BG rectangles
- (2) 2½" (6.4cm) White BG squares

3. Referring to the diagram for placement and orientation of the HST units, join in this order (1) 2" x 2½" (5.1cm x 6.4cm) White BG rectangle, (2) 2½ (7.6cm) White BG/Teal HST units, (1) 1½" x 2½" (6.4cm) Teal rectangle, (2) 2½ (6.4cm) White BG/Teal HST units, and (1) 2" x 2½ (5.1cm x 6.4cm) White BG rectangle to make the stem.

4. Referring to the diagrams for placement and orientation of units, join the 2½" (6.4cm) HST and CF units in rows of six as follows:

Row 1: (1) Red/White BG HST unit, (2) Light Red/Teal HST units, (2) Red/Teal HST units, and (1) Light Pink/White BG HST unit

Row 2: (2) Light Red/Bright White CF units (single Bright White corner), (2) Red/Bright White CF units (single Bright White corner), (1) Light Red/Bright White CF unit (double Bright White corners), (1) Red/Bright White CF unit (double Bright White corners)

Row 3: (1) Red/Bright White CF unit (double Bright White corners), (3) Light Red/Bright White CF units (single Bright White corner), (2) Red/Bright White CF units (single Bright White corner)

Row 4: (1) Light Red/White BG HST unit, (2) Red/Bright White CF units (single Bright White corner), (2) Light Red/Bright White CF units (single Bright White corner), (1) Red/White BG HST unit

Row 5: (2) 2½" (6.4cm) White BG squares, (1) Light Red/White BG HST unit, (1) Red/Bright White CF unit (double Bright White corners), (1) Light Red/Bright White CF unit (single Bright White corner), (1) Red/White BG HST

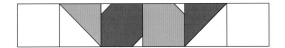

5. Join the rows and press. Note: The seams for the stem row and strawberry row do not match up. Make 3 Strawberry blocks.

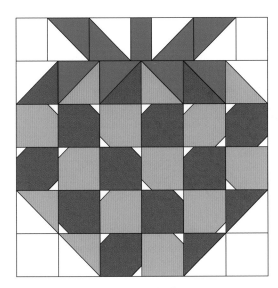

Strawberry Block
(Make 3)

Raspberry Block

Block size: 12½" (31.8cm) (Make 3)
Press the seams, taking care to nest seams by alternating directions. Seams that don't need nesting can be pressed in either direction.

UNIT ASSEMBLY

1. Following the HST instructions on page 8, make the following HST units from 3½" (8.9cm) squares. Press seams open and trim to 2½" (6.4cm) square. Note: Some units will not be used.
- (6) Purple/White BG units from (3) squares each
- (6) Light Purple/White BG units from (3) squares each
- (3) Purple/Light Teal units from (2) squares each
- (3) Light Purple/Light Teal units from (2) squares each
- (6) Light Teal/White BG units from (3) squares each

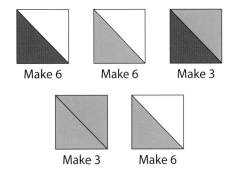

Make 6   Make 6   Make 3

Make 3   Make 6

2. Following the Corner Flip (CF) instructions on page 10, make the following CF units. Press seams open. Do not square.
- (9) 2½" (6.4cm) Purple/Bright White CF units from (9) 2½" (6.4cm) Purple squares and (9) 1" (2.5cm) Bright White squares, joining (1) Bright White square on the corner of each Purple square
- (6) 2½" (7.6cm) Purple/Bright White CF units from (6) 2½" (7.6cm) Purple squares and (12) 1" (2.5cm) Bright White squares, joining (2) Bright White squares on opposite corners of each Purple square

Make 9   Make 6

- (12) 2½" (6.4cm) Light Purple/ Bright White CF units from (12) 2½" (6.4cm) Light Purple squares and (12) 1" (2.5cm) Bright White squares, joining (1) Bright White square on the corner of each Light Purple square

Make 12

- (3) 2½" (6.4cm) Light Purple/ Bright White CF units from (3) 2½" (6.4cm) Light Purple squares and (6) 1" (2.5cm) Bright White squares, joining (2) Bright White squares on opposite corners of each Light Purple square

Make 3

- (3) 1½" x 2½" (3.8cm x 6.4cm) Purple/White CF units from (3) 1½" x 2½" (3.8cm x 6.4cm) Purple horizontal rectangles and (3) 1½" (3.8cm) White BG squares, joining (1) White BG square on the bottom right corner of each Purple horizontal rectangle

- (3) 1½" x 2½" (3.8cm x 6.4cm) Light Purple/ White BG CF units from (3) 1½" x 2½" (3.8cm x 6.4cm) Light Purple horizontal rectangles and (3) 1½" (3.8cm) White BG squares, joining (1) White BG square on the bottom left corner of each Light Purple horizontal rectangle.

Make 3 of Each

BLOCK ASSEMBLY

Each block uses:
- (5) 2½" (6.4cm) Purple/Bright White CF units
- (5) 2½" (6.4cm) Light Purple/Bright White CF units
- (1) 1½" x 2½" (3.9cm x 6.4cm) Purple/White BG CF unit
- (1) 1½" x 2½" (3.9cm x 6.4cm) Light Purple/White BG CF unit
- (2) 2½" (6.4cm) Purple/White BG HST units
- (2) 2½" (6.4cm) Light Purple/White BG HST units
- (1) 2½" (6.4cm) Purple/Light Teal HST unit
- (1) 2½" (6.4cm) Light Purple/Light Teal HST unit
- (2) 2½" (6.4cm) Light Teal/White BG HST units
- (1) 1" x 2½" (2.5cm x 6.4cm) Light Teal rectangle
- (2) 1½" x 2½" (3.9cm x 6.4cm) White BG rectangles
- (1) 1½" x 8½" (3.2cm x 21.6cm) White BG rectangle
- (2) 2½" x 10½" (7.6cm x 26.7cm) White BG rectangles
- (2) 2½" x 4¼" (6.4cm x 11.4cm) White BG rectangles

3. Referring to the Raspberry Block Assembly Diagram, join (2) 2½" x 4½" (6.4cm x 11.4cm) White BG rectangles, (2) 2½" (6.4cm) Light Teal/White BG HST units, and (1) 1" x 2½" (2.5cm x 6.4cm) Light Teal rectangle for the stem.

4. Arrange the 2½" (6.4cm) HST units, the CF units, and white rectangles into rows as follows, noting the placement and color orientation of the units:

Row 1: (1) Purple/White HST, (1) Light Teal/Light Purple HST, (1) Purple/Light Teal HST, (1) Light Purple/White BG HST

Row 2: (1) Light Purple/Bright White CF unit (double white corners), (1) Purple/Bright White CF unit (single white corner), (1) Light Purple/Bright White CF unit (single white corner), (1) Purple/Bright White (double white corner)

Row 3: (2) Purple/Bright White CF units (single white corner), (2) Light Purple/Bright White (single white corners)

Row 4: (1) Light Purple/White BG HST, (1) Purple/Bright White CF unit (double white corners), (1) Light Purple/Bright White CF unit (single white corners), (1) Purple/White BG HST

Row 5: (2) 1½" x 2½" (3.8cm x 6.4cm) White BG rectangles, (1) 1½" x 2½" (3.8cm x 6.4cm) Purple/White BG CF unit, (1) Light Purple/White BG CF unit

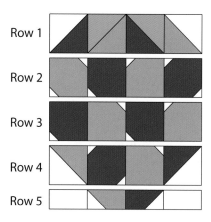

Row 1
Row 2
Row 3
Row 4
Row 5

5. Join the rows, adding (1) 1½" x 8½" (3.8cm x 21.6cm) White rectangle along the bottom. Sew (1) 2½" x 10½" (6.4cm x 26.7cm) White strip on the left and right sides of the unit. Sew the stem unit to the top. Note: Top stem seams and raspberry seams do not match up. Make 3. For this particular block, be sure to square to 12½".

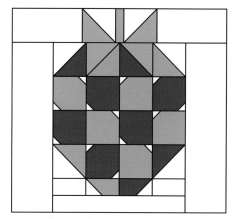

Raspberry Block Assembly Diagram
(Make 3)

Watermelon Block

Block size: 12½" (31.8cm) (Make 3)

UNIT ASSEMBLY

1. Following the Half Square Triangle (HST) instructions on page 8, make (6) 2½" (6.4cm) Green/White BG HST units from (3) 3½" (8.9cm) squares each of Green and White BG.

Make 3

2. Following the Corner Flip instructions on page 10, make the following CF units, pressing seams open.

- (6) Green/White BG/Pink HST/CF units from (6) 2½" (6.4cm) Green/White BG HST units and (6) 1½" (3.8cm) Pink squares, joining a small pink square on one Green corner of each Green/White BG HST unit
- (3) 2½" x 3½" (6.4cm x 8.9cm) White/Pink CF units from (3) 2½" x 3½" (6.4cm x 8.9cm) White horizontal rectangles and (6) 1" (2.5cm) Pink squares, joining (1) pink square in the bottom right and left corners of each white rectangle

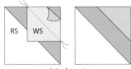

Make 6   Make 3

- (15) 2½" (6.4cm) Pink/Black CF units from (15) 2½" (6.4cm) Pink squares and (15) 1" (2.5cm) Black squares, joining a black square to a corner of each Pink square
- (9) 2½" (6.4cm) Light Pink/Black CF units from (9) 2½" (6.4cm) Light Pink squares and (9) 1" (2.5cm) Black squares, joining the Black square to one corner of each Light Pink square
- (6) 2½" (6.4cm) Light Pink/Black CF units from (6) 2½" (6.4cm) Light Pink squares and (12) 1" (2.5cm) Black squares, sewing (2) Black squares in opposite corners of each Light Pink square

Make 15   Make 15

BLOCK ASSEMBLY

Each block uses:

- (5) 2½" (6.4cm) Pink/Black CF units
- (5) 2½" (6.4cm) Light Pink/Black CF units
- (1) 2½" x 3½" (6.4cm x 8.9cm) BG/Pink CF unit
- (2) 2½" (6.4cm) White BG/Green/Pink HST/CF units
- (1) 1½" x 2½" (3.8cm x 6.4cm) Light Pink rectangle
- (2) 1½" x 6½" (3.8cm x 16.5cm) Pink rectangles
- (1) 1½" x 8½" (3.2cm x 21.6cm) Pink rectangle

- (2) 1½" x 6½" (3.8cm x 16.5cm) Green rectangles
- (1) 1½" x 8½" (3.2cm x 21.6cm) Green rectangle
- (2) 2½" x 12½" (6.4cm x 31.8cm) BG rectangles

3. Referring to the diagram, join the units in sections as follows. For Sections 1 and 2, join the units in columns, then join the columns together. Press seams, taking care to nest seams by pressing in alternating directions. Seams that don't need nesting can be pressed in either direction.

Section 1: (1) 1½" x 2½" (3.9cm x 6.4cm) Light Pink rectangle, (1) 2½" x 3½" (6.4cm x 8.9cm) BG/Pink CF unit, (2) 2½" (6.4cm) Light Pink/Black CF units (double black corners), (2) 2½" (6.4cm) Pink/Black CF units (single black corners)

Section 2: (3) 2½" (6.4cm) Pink/Black CF units (single black corners) and (3) 2½" (6.4cm) Light Pink/Black CF units, noting the placement of the black corners

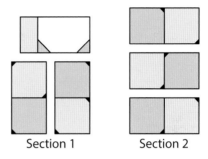

Section 1   Section 2

Section 3: Join (1) 1½" x 8½" (3.2cm x 21.6cm) Green rectangle and (1) 1½" x 8½" (3.2cm x 21.6cm) Pink rectangle. Join (1) 2½" (6.4cm) White BG/Green/Pink HST/CF unit to either side of the Pink/Green strip set

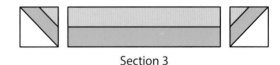

Section 3

4. Referring to the Watermelon Block Assembly Diagram, join the sections. Sew (1) 2½" x 12½" (6.4cm x 31.8cm) White rectangle to the top and bottom of the Pink/Green unit to complete the block and press. Make 3 blocks.

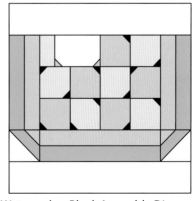

Watermelon Block Assembly Diagram
(Make 3)

Cherry Block

Block size: 12½" (31.8cm) (Make 3)

UNIT ASSEMBLY

1. Following the Half Square Triangle (HST) instructions on page 8, make (12) 2½" (6.4cm) Light Green/White BG HST units from (6) 3½" (8.9) squares each of Light Green and White BG.

Make 12

2. Following the Corner Flip (CF) instructions on page 10, make the following CF units, pressing the seams open.

- (12) 2½" (6.4cm) Maroon/ White BG CF units from (12) 2½" (6.4cm) Maroon squares and (12) 1½" (3.9cm) White BG squares, joining (1) White square to a corner of each Maroon square

Make 12

- (12) 2½" (6.4cm) Light Maroon/ White BG CF units from (12) 2½" (6.4cm) Light Maroon squares and (12) 1½" (3.9cm) White BG squares, joining a White square to one corner of each Light Maroon square

Make 12

- (6) 2½" (6.4cm) Light Green/White CF units from (6) 2½" (6.4cm) Light Green squares and (12) 2" (5.1cm) White squares, joining (2) White squares on opposite corners of each Light Green square

Make 6

BLOCK ASSEMBLY

Refer to the Cherry Block Assembly Diagram throughout assembly.

Cherry Block requires:
- (4) 2½" (6.4cm) Maroon/White BG CF units
- (4) 2½" (6.4cm) Light Maroon/White BG CF units
- (2) 2½" (6.4cm) Light Green/White BG CF units
- (4) 2½" (6.4cm) Light Green/White BG HST units
- (1) 1½" x 4½" Light Green rectangle
- (2) 2½" (6.4cm) White BG squares
- (2) 2" x 2½" (5.1cm x 6.4cm) White BG rectangles
- (2) 2½" x 6" (6.4cm x 15.2cm) White BG rectangles
- (2) 2½" x 6½" (6.4cm x 16.5cm) White BG rectangles
- (1) 2½" x 12½" (6.4cm x 31.8cm) BG rectangle

1. Join (2) 3½" (8.9cm) Light Green/White BG HST units with green sides facing. Make 2 units. Sew (1) 2" x 2½" (5.1cm x 6.4cm) White BG rectangle to the left side of the unit and (1) 2½" x 6½" (6.4cm x 16.5cm) White BG rectangle to the top. Make 2 units. Sew (1) unit to either side (1) 1½" x 4½" (3.8cm x 11.4cm) Light Green rectangle.

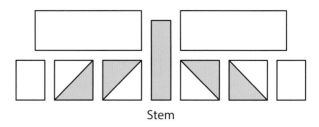

Stem

2. Referring to the Cherry Block Assembly Diagram, join the following units in columns as shown, noting the orientation of the CF units.

Column 1: (1) 2½" (6.4cm) White square, (1) 2½" (6.4cm) Maroon/White BG CF unit, and (1) 2½" (6.4cm) Light Maroon/White BG

Column 2: (1) 2½" (6.4cm) Green/White CF unit, (1) 2½" (6.4cm) Light Maroon/White BG, and (1) 2½" (6.4cm) Maroon/White BG CF unit

Column 3: (1) 2½" (6.4cm) Light Green/White CF unit, (1) 2½" (6.4cm) Maroon/White BG CF unit, and (1) 2½" (6.4cm) Light Maroon/White BG

Column 4: (1) 2½" (6.4cm) White square, (1) 2½" (6.4cm) Light Maroon/White BG, and (1) 2½" (6.4cm) Maroon/White BG CF unit

3. Join the columns, then sew (1) 2½" x 6½" (6.4cm x 16.5cm) White BG rectangle to either side and (1) 2½" x 12½" (6.4cm x 31.8cm) White BG rectangle along the bottom.

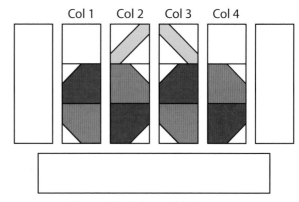

Cherry Block Assembly Diagram

4. Join the sections to complete the block. Make 3 blocks. The leaf seams are not meant to match up with the seams below. For this particular block, be sure to square to 12½".

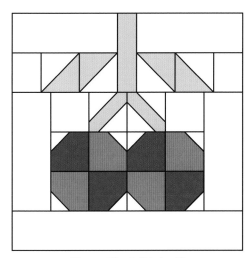

Cherry Block (Make 3)

Finishing the Quilt Top

1. Referring to the Quilt Top Assembly Diagram, join the blocks in rows of three as shown, then join the rows.

2. After trimming off the selvedge edges, join (2) 2½" (6.4cm) x WOF borders end to end and press. Repeat to make (2) long borders. Stitch the long borders to the sides of the quilt top. Trim to fit and press. Sew (1) 2½" (6.4cm) x WOF White border to the top and bottom of the quilt. Trim to fit and press.

3. Layer the quilt top, batting, and backing; baste. Quilt as desired.

4. Bind the quilt.

Quilt Top Assembly Diagram

Summer's Delight

Remembering my young kid's sticky fingers and cherry-stained tongues is one my sweetest summer memories. This delicious quilt uses a variety of blocks that create three giant freezer pops—one of my favorite summer treats. The quilt is a great size for a seasonal wall hanging or baby quilt.

Finished Size: 36" x 46" (91.4cm x 117cm)
Designed and quilted by Sherilyn Mortensen
Pieced by Jacqueline Pyne
Quilt bound by Amy Maxfield
Fabric: Moda Grunge

Fabric Requirements
- 5" x 12" (12.7cm x 30.5cm) each of Dark Pink, Medium Pink, Dark Brown, Medium Brown, Dark Orange, and Medium Orange
- 3" x 24" (7.6cm x 61cm) each of Pink, Brown, and Orange
- 7" x 15" (17.8cm x 38.1cm) Light Pink
- 7" x 13" (17.8cm x 33cm) Light Brown
- 7" x 14" (17.8cm x 35.6cm) Light Orange
- 3" (7.6cm) x width of fabric (WOF) tan
- 1 yard (0.9m) White Background fabric
- 2¾ yards (2.5m) Backing fabric
- ⅓ yard (0.3m) Binding material

Cutting Instructions

From Dark Pink fabric, cut:
- (1) 4½" x 6½" (11.4cm x 16.5cm) rectangle
- (1) 4½" (11.4cm) square

From Medium Pink fabric, cut:
- (1) 4½" x 6½" (11.4cm x 16.5cm) rectangle
- (1) 4½" (11.4cm) square

From Pink fabric, cut:
- (2) 2½" x 6½" (6.4cm x 16.5cm) rectangles
- (2) 2½" x 4½" (6.4cm x 11.4cm) rectangles

From Light Pink fabric, cut:
- (1) 6½" (16.5cm) square
- (1) 4½" x 6½" (11.4cm x 16.5cm) rectangle

From Dark Brown fabric, cut:
- (1) 4½" x 6½" (11.4cm x 16.5cm) rectangle
- (1) 4½" (11.4cm) square

From Medium Brown fabric, cut:
- (1) 4½" x 6½" (11.4cm x 16.5cm) rectangle
- (1) 4½" (11.4cm) square

From Brown fabric, cut:
- (2) 2½" x 6½" (6.4cm x 16.5cm) rectangles
- (2) 2½" x 4½" (6.4cm x 11.4cm) rectangles

From Light Brown fabric, cut:
- (1) 2½" x 4½" (6.4cm x 11.4cm) rectangle
- (1) 2½" (6.4cm) square
- (1) 6½" (16.5cm) square

From Dark Orange fabric, cut:
- (1) 4½" x 6½" (11.4cm x 16.5cm) rectangle
- (1) 4½" (11.4cm) square

From Medium Orange fabric, cut:
- (1) 4½" x 6½" (11.4cm x 16.5cm) rectangle
- (1) 4½" (11.4cm) square

From Orange fabric, cut:
- (2) 2½" x 6½" (6.4cm x 16.5cm) rectangles
- (2) 2½" x 4½" (6.4cm x 11.4cm) rectangles

From Light Orange fabric, cut:
- (1) 6½" (16.5cm) square
- (1) 4½" x 6½" (11.4cm x 16.5cm) rectangle

From Tan fabric, cut:
- (3) 2½" (6.4cm) squares
- (3) 2½" x 10½" (6.4cm x 26.7cm) strips

From White Background fabric, cut:
- (8) 2½" (6.4cm) squares
- (2) 2½" x 4½" (6.4cm x 11.4cm) rectangles
- (2) 2½" x 8½" (6.4cm x 21.6cm) rectangles
- (4) 2½" x 10½" (6.4cm x 26.7cm) rectangles
- (2) 4½" (11.4cm) squares
- (1) 4½" x 6½" (11.4cm x 16.5cm) rectangle
- (2) 4½" x 12½" (11.4cm x 31.8cm) rectangles
- (4) 6½" x 12½" (16.5cm x 31.8cm) rectangles
- (4) 10½" x 12½" (26.7cm x 31.8cm) rectangles

Unit Assembly

1. Following the Corner Flip (CF) Technique instructions on page 10, make the following CF units, sewing the smaller square onto one corner of the larger unit and pressing the seams open.

- (1) 6½" (16.5cm) Light Pink/White BG CF Unit from (1) 6½" (16.5cm) light pink square and (1) 2½" (6.4cm) White BG square
- (1) 6½" (16.5cm) Light Brown/White BG CF unit from (1) 6½" (16.5cm) Light Brown square and (1) 2½" (6.4cm) White BG square
- (1) 4½" (11.4cm) White BG/Light Brown CF unit from (1) 4½" (11.4cm) White BG square and (1) 2½" (6.4cm) Light Brown square
- (1) 6½"(16.5cm) Light Orange/White BG CF unit from (1) 6½" (16.5cm) Light Orange square and (1) 2½" (6.4cm) White BG square

2. In the same manner as Step 1, make the following CF units, sewing the smaller square onto upper right corner of the larger vertical rectangle. Press the seams open.

- (1) 4½"x 6½" (11.4cm x 16.5cm) Light Pink/White BG CF unit from (1) 4½" x 6½" (11.4cm x 16.5cm) Light Pink rectangle and 2½" (6.4cm) White BG square
- (1) 4½" x 6½" (11.4cm x 16.5cm) Light Orange/White BG CF unit from (1) 4½" x 6½" (11.4cm x 16.5cm) Light Orange vertical rectangle and (1) 2½" (6.4cm) White BG square

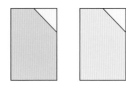

Block Assembly

Refer to the individual block diagrams throughout assembly. Press as desired, taking care to nest the seams by alternating pressing directions. Note: Seams that don't need nesting can be pressed in either direction.

BLOCK A
Block size: 12½" (31.8cm) square (Make 1)

1. Join (1) 2½" x 6½" (6.4cm x 16.5cm) Pink rectangle, (1) 6½" (16.5cm) Light Pink/White BG CF unit and (1) 4½" x 6½" (11.4cm x 16.5cm) White BG rectangle as shown. Sew (1) 6½" x 12½" (16.5cm x 31.8cm) White BG rectangle to the left side of the unit.

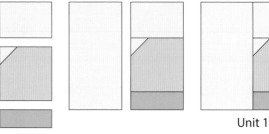

Unit 1

Block A

BLOCK B
Block size: 12½" (31.8cm) square (Make 1)

1. Join (1) 2½" x 4½" (6.4cm x 11.4cm) Pink rectangle and (1) 4½" x 6½" (11.4cm x 16.5cm) Light Pink/White BG CF unit. Sew (1) 2½" x 8½" (6.4cm x 21.6cm) White BG strip on the right side of the CF unit.

2. Join (1) 2½" x 6½" (6.4cm x 16.5cm) Brown rectangle and (1) 6½" (16.5cm) square Light Brown/White BG CF unit.

3. Join the Light Brown/White BG CF unit and the Pink CF unit. Sew (1) 4½" x 12½" (11.4cm x 31.8cm) White BG rectangle to the top of the units to complete the block.

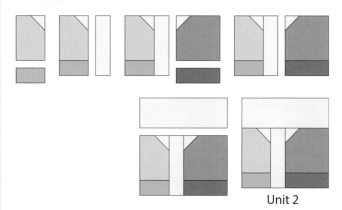

Unit 2

Block B

BLOCK C
Block size: 12½" (31.8cm) square (Make 1)

1. Join (1) 2½" x 4½" (6.4cm x 11.4cm) Brown rectangle, (1) 2½" x 4½" (6.4cm x 11.4cm) Light Brown rectangle, and 4½" (6.4cm) White BG/Light Brown CF unit. Sew (1) 2½" x 8½" (6.4cm x 21.6cm) White BG strip along the right side of the unit.

2. Join the 2½" x 6½" (6.4cm x 16.5cm) Orange rectangle and 6½" (16.5cm) Light Orange/White BG CF Unit.

3. Join the units, then sew (1) 4½" x 12½" (11.4cm x 31.8cm) White BG rectangle along the top.

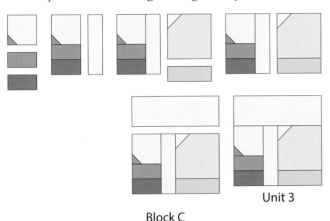

Unit 3

Block C

BLOCK D
Block size: 10½" x 12½" (26.7cm x 31.8cm) (Make 1)

1. Join (1) 2½" x 4½" (6.4cm x 11.4cm) Orange rectangle, the 4½" x 6½" (11.4cm x 16.5cm) Light Orange/White BG CF unit, and (1) 4½" (6.4cm) White BG square. Sew the 6½" x 12½" (16.5cm x 31.8cm) White BG rectangle along the right side.

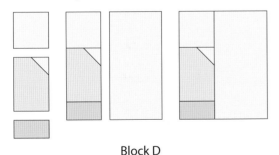

Block D

ROW 1

1. Join Blocks A–D as shown to form Row 1.

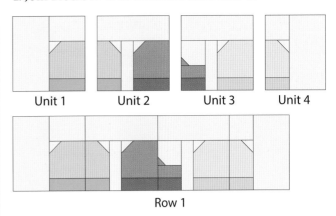

Unit 1   Unit 2   Unit 3   Unit 4

Row 1

BLOCK E
Block size: 12½" (31.8cm) square (Make 1)

1. Join (1) 2½" (6.4cm) Tan square and (1) 2½" x 4½" (6.4cm x 11.4cm) White BG rectangle.

2. Referring to the diagram, join the Tan/White BG unit, (1) 4½" x 6½" (11.4cm x 16.5cm) Dark Pink rectangle, (1) 4½" x 6½" (11.4cm x 16.5cm) Medium Pink rectangle, and (1) 2½" x 6½" (6.4cm x 16.5cm) Pink rectangle.

3. Sew (1) 6½" x 12½" (16.5cm x 31.8cm) White BG rectangle along the left side.

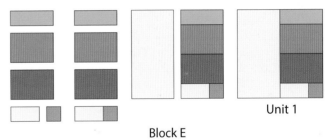

Unit 1

Block E

BLOCK F
Block size: 12½" (31.8cm) square (Make 1)

1. Join (1) 4½" (6.4cm) Dark Pink square, (1) 4½" (6.4cm) Medium Pink square, and (1) 2½" x 4½" (6.4cm x 11.4cm) Pink rectangle as shown. Sew (1) 2½" x 10½" (6.4cm x 26.7cm) White BG rectangle along the right side.

2. Join (1) 4½" x 6½" (11.4cm x 16.5cm) Dark Brown rectangle, (1) 4½" x 6½" (11.4cm x 16.5cm) Medium Brown rectangle, and (1) 2½" x 6½" (6.4cm x 16.5cm) Brown rectangle. Sew the units together.

3. Join (1) 2½" x 10½" (6.4cm x 26.7cm) White BG rectangle and (1) 2½" (6.4cm) Tan square. Sew the White BG/Tan rectangle along the bottom of the unit.

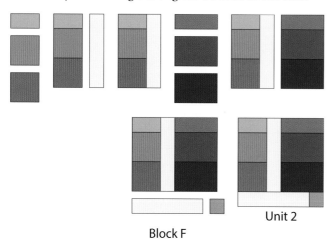

Block F

BLOCK G
Block size: 12½" (31.8cm) square (Make 1)

1. Join (1) 4½" (6.4cm) Dark Brown square, (1) 4½" (6.4cm) Medium Brown square, and (1) 2½" x 4½" (6.4cm x 11.4cm) Brown rectangle as shown. Sew (1) 2½" x 10½" (6.4cm x 26.7cm) White BG rectangle along the right side.

2. Join (1) 4½" x 6½" (11.4cm x 16.5cm) Dark Orange rectangle, (1) 4½" x 6½" (11.4cm x 16.5cm) Medium Orange rectangle, and (1) 2½" x 6½" (6.4cm x 16.5cm) Orange rectangle. Join the units.

3. Join (1) 2½" x 10½" (6.4cm x 26.7cm) White BG rectangle and (1) 2½" (6.4cm) Tan square. Sew the White BG/Tan unit along the bottom of the Orange/Brown unit.

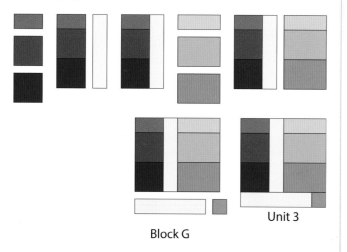

Unit 3

Block G

BLOCK H
Block size: 10½" x 12½" (26.7cm x 31.8cm) (Make 1)

1. Join (1) 4½" (6.4cm) Dark Orange square, (1) 4½" (6.4cm) Medium Orange square, (1) 2½" x 4½" (6.4cm x 11.4cm) Orange rectangle, and (1) 2½" x 4½" (6.4cm x 11.4cm) White BG rectangle.

2. Sew (1) 6½" x 12½" (16.5cm x 31.8cm) White BG rectangle along the right side.

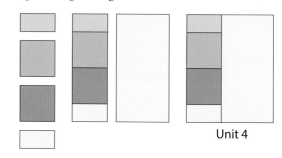

Unit 4

Block H

ROW 2

1. Join Blocks E–H together to form Row 2.

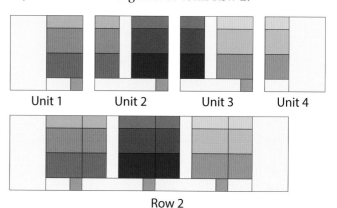

Unit 1   Unit 2   Unit 3   Unit 4

Row 2

BLOCK I/ROW 3
Block size: 12½" (31.8cm) square (Make 3)

1. Join (1) 2½" x 10½" (6.4cm x 26.7cm) Tan rectangle and (1) 2½" (6.4cm) White BG square. Sew the White BG/Tan unit to the right-hand side of (1) 10½" x 12½" (26.7cm x 31.8cm) White BG rectangle. Make 3 units.

2. Sew the units together. Join (1) 10½" x 12½" (26.7cm x 31.8cm) White BG rectangle to the right side of the unit to form Row 3.

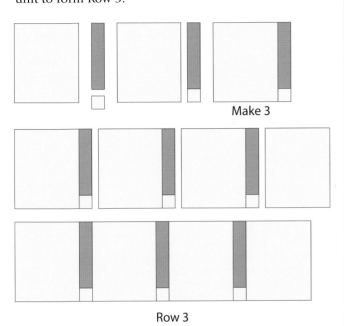

Make 3

Row 3

Finishing the Quilt Top

1. Join the rows to complete the quilt top.

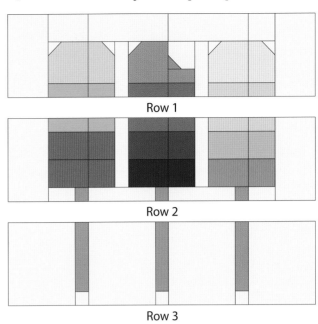

Row 1

Row 2

Row 3

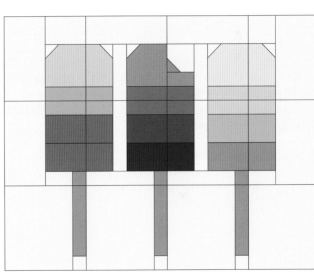

Quilt Assembly Diagram

2. Layer the quilt top, batting, and backing; baste. Quilt as desired.

3. Bind the quilt.

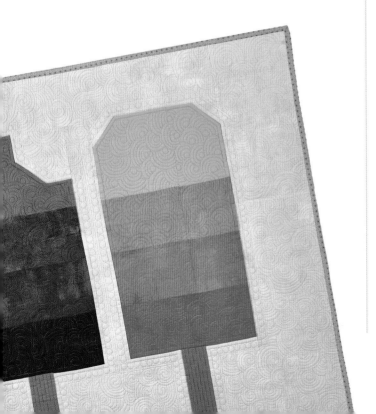

Liberty

My patriotism and pride for my country runs deep as I'm sure it does for many around the world! Celebrate liberty with this bright and beautiful stars and stripes quilt top. Hang it as a banner or proudly display it on a table as a runner.

Finished Size: 16"x 64" (40.6cm x 162.6cm)
Designed, pieced, and quilted by Sherilyn Mortensen
Fabric: Kona solids, Elizabeth Hartman, stash

Fabric Requirements
- ⅓ yard (0.3m) Navy
- ¼ yard (0.2m) each Aqua and Red
- ⅛ yard (0.1m) Light Aqua
- ⅛ yard (0.1m) White
- 6" (15.2cm) x width of fabric (WOF) Dark Red
- 1 yard (0.9m) Off-White Background fabric
- 2¾ yards (2.5m) Backing fabric
- ⅓ yard (0.3m) Binding fabric

Cutting Instructions

From Navy fabric, cut:
- (2) 4" (10.2cm) squares
- (20) 3½" (8.9cm) squares

From Aqua fabric, cut:
- (2) 4" (10.2cm) squares
- (8) 3½" (8.9cm) squares
- (8) 2½" (6.5cm) squares

From Light Aqua fabric, cut:
- (4) 4" (10.2cm) squares
- (4) 2½" (6.5cm) squares

From the White fabric, cut:
- (6) 3½" (8.9cm) squares

From Red fabric, cut:
- (4) 4" (10.2cm) squares
- (14) 3½" (8.9cm) squares

From Dark Red fabric, cut:
- (4) 2½" x 12½" (6.5cm x 31.8cm) rectangles

From Off-White Background fabric, cut:
- (24) 3½" (8.9cm) squares
- (12) 2½" (6.5cm) squares
- (2) 2½" x 12½" (6.5cm x 31.8cm) rectangles
- (4) 3½" x 12½" (8.9cm x 31.8cm) rectangles
- (4) 2½" x width of fabric (WOF) strips

Unit Assembly

1. Following the Half Square Triangle (HST) instructions on page 8, make the following HST units from 3½" (8.9cm) squares. Press seams open and trim to 2½" (6.5cm) square.
- (16) Navy/Off-White BG HST units from (8) squares each
- (16) Aqua/Off-White BG HST units from (8) squares
- (16) Red/Off-White BG HST units from (8) 3½" (8.9cm) squares each
- (4) Red/White HST units from (2) squares each
- (8) Navy/White HST units from (4) squares each

Make 16

Make 16

Make 16

Make 4

Make 8

2. Make the following HST units from 4" (10.2cm) squares, pressing seams open. Do not square. These units will be used to make QHST units.
- (4) Navy/Light Aqua units from (2) squares each
- (4) Red/Aqua units from (2) squares each
- (4) Red/Light Aqua units from (2) each

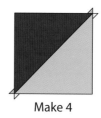
Make 4

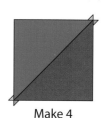
Make 4

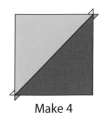
Make 4

3. Following the Quarter Half Square Triangle (QHST) instructions on page 9, make the following QHST units, noting the orientation of the colors when piecing the units. Press seams open and trim to 2½" (6.5cm) square:

- (8) Navy/Light Aqua/Red QHST units from (4) 3½" (8.9cm) Navy/Light Aqua HST units (not squared) and (4) 3½" (8.9cm) Red squares
- (8) Red/Aqua/Navy QHST units from (4) 3½" (8.9cm) Red/Aqua HST units (not squared) and (4) 3½" (8.9cm) Navy squares
- (8) Red/Light Aqua/Navy QHST units from (4) 3½" (8.9cm) Red/Light Aqua HST units (not squared) and (4) 3½" (8.9cm) Navy squares

Make 4 of Each

Star Block Assembly

Block size: 12½" (31.8cm) square
All Star blocks are assembled in the same way. Refer to the Star Block Assembly Diagram throughout assembly. Make (1) block each in Navy, Aqua, and Red. Press seams as desired, taking care to nest the seams by pressing in the opposite directions.

For each Navy Star Block, you will need:
- (16) 2½" (6.5cm) Navy/Off-White BG HST units
- (4) 2½" (6.5cm) Red/White HST units
- (8) 2½" (6.5cm) Navy/Light Aqua/Red QHST units
- (4) 2½" (6.5cm) Aqua squares
- (4) 2½" (6.5cm) Off-White BG squares

1. Sew the units together in rows as follows:
Row 1: (1) 2½" (6.5cm) Off-White BG square and (2) 2½" (6.5cm) Navy/Off-White BG HST units
Row 2: (1) 2½" (6.5cm) Navy/Off-White BG HST unit, (1) 2½" (6.5cm) Aqua square, and (1) 2½" (6.5cm) Navy/Light Aqua/Red QHST unit
Row 3: (1) 2½" (6.5cm) Navy/Off-White BG HST unit, (1) 2½" (6.5cm) Navy/Light Aqua/Red QHST unit, and (1) 2½" (6.5cm) Red/White HST unit

2. Sew the rows together to form a section. Make (4) sections.

3. Join the sections to complete the Star block, noting the orientation of the points. Take care to nest the seams as you join the rows.

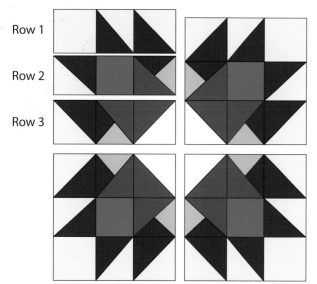

Star Block Assembly Diagram

Navy Star Block (Make 1)

4. In the same manner, make (1) Aqua Star Block and (1) Red Star Block.

To make an Aqua Star Block, you will need:
- (16) 2½" (6.5cm) Aqua/Off-White BG HST units
- (4) 2½" (6.5cm) Navy/White HST units
- (8) 2½" (6.5cm) Red/Aqua/Navy QHST units
- (4) 2½" (6.5cm) Light Aqua squares
- (4) 2½" (6.5cm) Off-White BG squares

Aqua Star Block (Make 1)

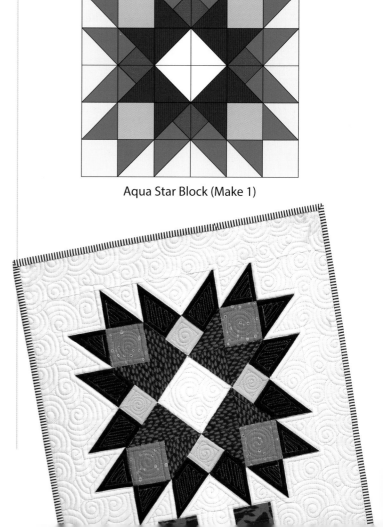

To make a Red Star Block, you will need:

- (16) 2½" (6.5cm) Red/Off-White BG HST units
- (4) 2½" (6.5cm) Navy/White HST units
- (8) 2½" (6.5cm) Red/Light Aqua/Navy QHST units
- (4) 2½" (6.5cm) Aqua squares
- (4) 2½" (6.5cm) Off-White BG squares

Red Star Block (Make 1)

Red & White Stripe Block

Block size: 12½" (31.8cm) square (Make 2)

For each block, you will need:

- (2) 3½" x 12½" (8.9cm x 31.8cm) Off-White BG rectangles
- (1) 2½" x 12½" (6.5cm x 31.8cm) Off-White BG rectangle
- (2) 2½" x 12½" (6.5cm x 31.8cm) Dark Red rectangles

1. Referring to the diagram, join (2) 3½" x 12½" (8.9cm x 31.8cm) Off-White BG rectangles, (2) 2½" x 12½" (6.5cm x 31.8cm) Dark Red rectangles, and (1) 2½" x 12½" (6.5cm x 31.8cm) Off-White BG rectangle, alternating the placement of the rectangles as shown. Press the seams. Make 2 blocks.

Make 2

Finishing

1. Referring to the Liberty Runner Assembly Diagram, join the blocks alternating the Star Blocks and Red and White Striped Blocks. Press the seams.

2. After removing the selvedge edges, cut (1) 2½" (6.5cm) x WOF background border strip in half horizontally. Join (1) half background fabric border strip to (1) 2½" (6.5cm) x WOF background border strips and press. Repeat to make (2) long border strips. Join the long borders to the long sides of the runner. Trim to fit and press. Cut (1) 2½" (6.5cm) x WOF background border strip in half horizontally. Join one half to each end of the runner, then trim to fit and press.

Liberty Runner Assembly Diagram

3. Layer the backing, batting, and quilt top; baste. Quilt as desired.

4. Bind the quilt.

Freedom

Twenty blocks make up this beautiful and generously sized throw. The contrasting colors compete and complement just enough to reflect the striking angular design. Swap out the colors to reflect your own style and representation.

60" x 75" (152.4cm x 190.5cm)
Designed and quilted by Sherilyn Mortensen
Pieced by Deborah Russell
Quilt bound by Amy Maxfield
Fabric: Kona solids, stash

Fabric Requirements
- 2 yards (1.8m) each Aqua, Navy, Mint, Red, and Sky Blue
- 4⅓ yards (3.9m) Backing fabric
- 20" (50.8cm) Width of Fabric (WOF) Binding fabric

Cutting Instructions:

From Aqua and Red fabrics, cut:
- (16) 3" (7.6cm) squares
- (64) 4" (10.2cm) squares
- (24) 6½" (16.5cm) squares

From Navy and Sky Blue fabrics, cut:
- (48) 3" (7.6cm) square
- (64) 4" (10.2cm) squares
- (8) 6½" (16.5cm) squares

From Mint fabric, cut:
- (32) 3" (7.6cm) squares
- (64) 4" (10.2cm) squares
- (16) 6½" (16.5cm) squares

Unit Assembly

1. Following the Half Square Triangle (HST) directions on page 8, make the following HST units from 4" (10.2cm) squares. Press the seams open and trim to 3" (7.6cm) square.
- (64) Aqua/Navy units from (32) squares each
- (64) Mint/Aqua units from (32) squares each
- (64) Sky Blue/ Red units and (32) squares each
- (64) Red/Mint units from (32) squares each
- (64) Navy/Sky Blue units from (32) squares each

Make 64

Make 64

Make 64

Make 64

Make 64

2. Make the following 5½" (14cm) HST units from 6½" (16.5cm) squares, pressing seams open and trimming to 5½" (14cm) square.
- (16) Mint/Red units from (8) squares each
- (16) Red/Sky Blue units from (8) squares each
- (16) Mint/Aqua units from (8) squares each
- (16) Navy/Aqua units from (8) squares each
- (16) Red/Aqua units from (8) squares each

Make 16 of Each

3. Following the Corner Flip (CF) instructions on page 10, make the following CF blocks. Press the seams open.

- (16) Mint/Red/Sky Blue HST/ CF units from (16) 5½" (14cm) Mint/Red HST units and (16) 3" (8.9cm) Sky Blue squares, sewing the Sky Blue square on the Red corner of each HST

Make 16

- (16) Red/Sky Blue/Navy HST/CF units from (16) 5½" (14cm) Red/ Sky Blue HST units and (16) 3" (8.9cm) Navy squares, sewing the navy squares on the Sky Blue corner of the HST units

Make 16

- (16) Mint/Aqua/Navy HST/CF units from (16) 5½" (14cm) Mint/Aqua HST units and (16) 3" (8.9cm) Navy squares, sewing the Navy squares on the Aqua corners

Make 16

- (16) Navy/Aqua/Sky Blue HST/ CF units from (16) 5½" (14cm) Navy/Aqua HST units and (16) 3" (8.9cm) Sky Blue squares, sewing the Sky Blue squares on the Aqua corners

Make 16

- (16) Red/Aqua/Mint HST/CF units from (16) 5½" (14cm) Red/Aqua HST units and (16) 3" (8.9cm) Mint squares, sewing the Mint squares on the Aqua corners

Make 16

Freedom Block Assembly

Block size: 15½" (38.1cm) square (Make 20 blocks)
All of the Freedom blocks are assembled in the same manner. Take care to note the direction of the units when piecing the blocks. Make 4 blocks in each colorway, pressing seams open.

Refer to the Block A Assembly Diagram throughout assembly.

For each Block A, you will need:
- (4) 3" (7.6cm) Aqua squares
- (16) 3" (7.6cm) Aqua/Navy HST units
- (4) 5½" (14cm) Mint/Red/Sky Blue HST units

1. To make Block A, join (2) 3" (7.6cm) Aqua/Navy HST units with mirror facing; make 2 units. Sew (1) 3" (7.6cm) Aqua square to (1) 3" x 5½" (7.6cm x 14cm) Aqua/Navy HST unit for row 1. Sew (1) 3" x 5½" (7.6cm x 14cm) Aqua/Navy HST unit to (1) 5½" (14cm) Mint/ Red/Sky Blue HST/CF unit for row 2. Join the rows. Make (4) sections.

2. Referring to the diagram, join the (4) sections, pressing the seams open. Make (4) of Block A.

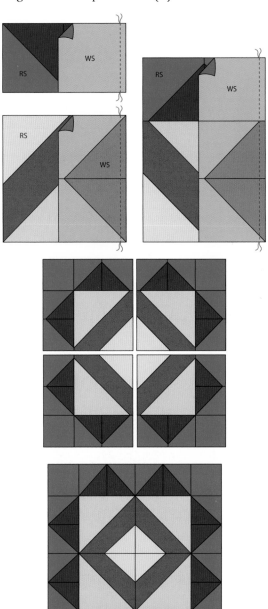

Block A Assembly Diagram
(Make 4)

3. In the same manner as Block A, make (4) each of Blocks B–E:

For each Block B, you will need:
- (4) 3" (7.6cm) Mint squares
- (16) 3" (7.6cm) Mint/Aqua HST units
- (4) 5½" (14cm) Red/Sky Blue/Navy HST/CF Units

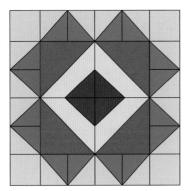

Block B (Make 4)

For each Block C, you will need:
- (4) 3" (7.6cm) Sky Blue squares
- (16) 3" (7.6cm) Sky Blue/Red HST units
- (4) 5½" (14cm) Mint/Aqua/Navy HST/CF units

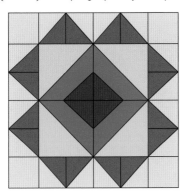

Block C (Make 4)

For each Block D, you will need:
- (4) 3" (7.6cm) Red squares
- (16) 3" (7.6cm) Red/Mint HST units
- (4) 5½" (14cm) Navy/Aqua/Sky Blue HST/CF units

Block D (Make 4)

For each Block E, you will need:
- (4) 3" (7.6cm) Navy squares
- (16) 3" (7.6cm) Navy/Sky Blue HST units
- (4) 5½" (14cm) Red/Aqua/Mint HST/CF units

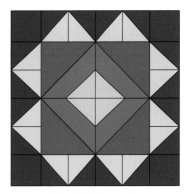

Block E (Make 4)

Finishing

1. Join the blocks in rows of four, alternating the colors as shown.

2. Layer the backing, batting, and quilt top; baste. Quilt as desired, then bind the quilt.

Follow the Sun

Sunflowers are some of my very favorite flowers—the bigger the better! Giant sunflowers stacked in neat rows make for a large, bright, and cheery throw quilt. This design calls for six sunflower blocks, six leaf blocks and a white border.

60" x 78" (152.4cm x 198.1cm)
Designed, pieced, and quilted by Sherilyn Mortensen
Quilt bound by Amy Maxfield
Fabric used: Moda Grunge, Tula Pink, stash

Fabric Requirements
- ¾ yard (0.7m) each Gold, Dark Yellow, and Lime Green
- ½ yard (0.5m) each Yellow and Light Yellow
- 1 yard (0.9m) Green
- 2 yards (1.8m) Dark Green
- ¼ yard (0.2m) Brown
- 3 yards (2.7m) White Background fabric
- 4½ yards (4.1m) Backing fabric
- 20" (50.8cm) x Width of Fabric (WOF) Binding fabric

Cutting Instructions

From Gold fabric, cut:
- (12) 3½" x 6½" (8.9cm x 16.5cm) rectangles
- (24) 4½" (11.4cm) squares

From Light Yellow fabric, cut:
- (12) 2" (5.1cm) squares
- (24) 4½" (11.4cm) squares

From Yellow fabric, cut:
- (12) 2" (5.1cm) squares
- (24) 4½" (11.4cm) squares

From Dark Yellow fabric, cut:
- (12) 3½" x 6½" (8.9cm x 16.5cm) rectangles
- (24) 4½" (11.4cm) squares

From Dark Green fabric, cut:
- (6) 2" x 18½" (5.1cm x 47cm) strips
- (18) 6½" x 7¼" (16.5cm x 18.4cm) rectangles
- (36) 5" (12.7cm) squares

From Green fabric, cut:
- (18) 6½" x 7¼" (16.5cm x 18.4cm) rectangles

From Lime Green fabric, cut:
- (36) 5" (12.7cm) squares

From Brown fabric, cut:
- (6) 6½" (16.5cm) squares

From White Background fabric, cut:
- (96) 3½" (8.9cm) squares
- (24) 4½" (11.4cm) squares
- (12) 2¼" x 18½" (5.7cm x 47cm) strips
- (8) 3½" x WOF strips for borders

Sunflower Block Assembly

1. Following the Half Square Triangles (HST) directions on page 8, make the following HST units from 4½" (11.4cm) squares. Press seams open and trim to 3½" (8.9cm) square.
- (24) Gold/White BG units from (12) squares each
- (24) Dark Yellow/White BG units from (12) squares each
- (24) Light Yellow/Gold units from (12) squares each
- (24) Dark Yellow/Yellow units from (12) squares each
- (24) Light Yellow/Yellow units from (12) squares each

Make 24 of Each

2. Following the Corner Flip (CF) instructions on page 10, make the following Corner Flip units. Press seams open.
- (3) 6½" (16.5cm) Brown/Light Yellow CF units from (3) 6½" (16.5cm) brown squares and (12) 2" (5.1cm) light yellow squares
- (3) 6½" (16.5cm) Brown/Yellow CF units from (3) 6½" (16.5cm) brown squares and (12) 2" (5.1cm) yellow squares

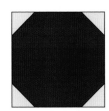

Make 3 of Each

Sunflower Block Assembly

Block sizes: 18½" (47cm) square

All of the Sunflower blocks are assembled in the same manner. Stitch and press the sections as desired, taking care to nest the seams by alternating pressing directions. Seams that don't need nesting can be pressed in either direction.

Each Sunflower Block A uses:
- (8) 3½" (8.9cm) Dark Yellow/White BG HST units
- (8) 3½" (8.9cm) Dark Yellow/Yellow HST units
- (4) 3½" (8.9cm) Light Yellow/Yellow HST units
- (1) 6½" (16.2cm) Brown/Yellow CF unit
- (4) 3½" (8.9cm) White BG squares
- (4) 3½" x 6½" (8.9cm x 16.2cm) Gold rectangles

3. Join (1) 3½" (8.9cm) White BG square and (1)3½" (8.9cm) Dark Yellow/White BG HST unit. Join (1)3½" (8.9cm) Dark Yellow/White HST unit and (1) 3½" (8.9cm) Light Yellow/Yellow HST unit. Sew the units together. Make 4 units.

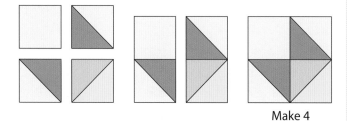

Make 4

4. Join (2) 3½" (8.9cm) Dark Yellow/Light Yellow HST units, light yellow sides together. Sew (1) 3½" x 6½" (8.9cm x 16.2cm) Gold rectangle to the bottom of the HST unit. Make 4 units.

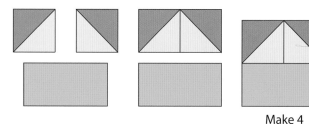

Make 4

5. Sew the units together in rows, including the center Brown/Yellow CF unit, alternating the blocks.

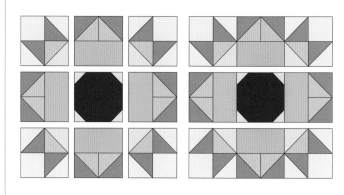

6. Join the rows to form Block A. Make 3 of Block A.

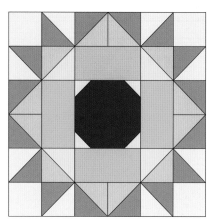

Sunflower Block A (Make 3)

7. In the same manner as above, make (3) of Block B.

Each Block B uses:
- (8) 3½" (8.9cm) Gold/White BG HST units
- (8) 3½" (8.9cm) Gold/Yellow HST units
- (4) 3½" (8.9cm) Light Yellow/Yellow HST units
- (1) 6½" (16.2cm) Brown/Light Yellow CF unit
- (4) 3½" (8.9cm) White BG squares
- (4) 3½" x 6½" (8.9cm x 16.2cm) Dark Yellow rectangles

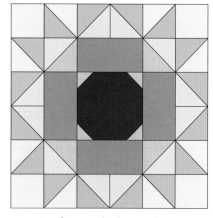

Sunflower Block B (Make 3)

Leaf Block Unit Assembly

Following the Corner Flip (CF) instructions on page 10, make the following block units. Refer to the diagram throughout assembly for placement and orientation of the units. Press seams open.

LEAF BLOCK UNIT 1

Each block uses:
- (12) 6½" x 7¼" (16.5cm x 18.4cm) Dark Green rectangles
- (24) 5" (12.7cm) Lime Green squares
- (24) 3½" (8.9cm) White BG squares
  Join (1) 5" (12.7cm) Lime Green square to the top right and bottom left corners of (1) 6½" x 7¼" (16.5cm x 18.4cm) Dark Green rectangle. Join (1) 3½" (8.9cm) White BG square to each of the Lime Green corners to complete the unit. Make 12 units.

Make 12

Leaf Block Unit 1

LEAF BLOCK UNIT 2

Each block uses:
- (6) 6½" x 7¼" (16.5cm x 18.4cm) Dark Green rectangles
- (12) 5" (12.7cm) Lime Green squares
- (12) 3½" (8.9cm) White BG squares
  Join (1) 5" (12.7cm) Lime Green square to the top left and bottom right corners of (1) 6½" x 7¼" (16.5cm x 18.4cm) Dark Green rectangle. Join (1) 3½" (8.9cm) White BG square to each of the Lime Green corners. Make 6 units.

Make 6

Leaf Block Unit 2

LEAF BLOCK UNIT 3

Each block uses:
- (6) 6½" x 7¼" (16.5cm x 18.4cm) Green rectangles
- (12) 5" (12.7cm) Dark Green squares
- (12) 3½" (8.9cm) White BG squares
  Join (1) 5" (12.7cm) Dark Green square to the top right and bottom left of a 6½" x 7¼" (16.5cm x 18.4cm) Green rectangle. Join a 3½" (8.9cm) White BG square to each Dark Green corner. Make 6 units.

  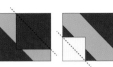

Make 6

Leaf Block Unit 3

LEAF BLOCK UNIT 4 (MAKE 6)

Each block uses:
- (12) 6½" x 7¼" (16.5cm x 18.4cm) Green rectangles
- (24) 5" (12.7cm) Dark Green squares
- (24) 3½" (8.9cm) White BG squares
  Join (1) 5" (12.7cm) Dark Green square to the top left and bottom right of (1) 6½" x 7¼" (16.5cm x 18.4cm) Green rectangle. Join (1) 3½" (8.9cm) White BG square to each Dark Green corner. Make 12 units.

Make 12

Leaf Block Unit 4

Leaf Block Assembly

Block size: 18½" (47cm) square

1. Referring to the diagram for placement and orientation, join the Leaf Blocks in columns as follows. Make 6 of each column.
Column 1: Join (1) each of Leaf Block Unit 1, Leaf Block Unit 4, and Leaf Block Unit 1
Column 2: Join (1) each of Leaf Block Unit 3, Leaf Block Unit 2, and Leaf Block Unit 3

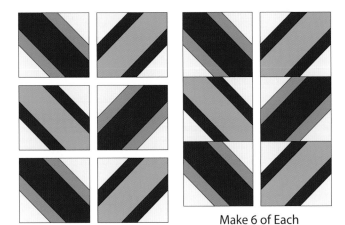

Column 1   Column 2   Make 6 of Each

2. Referring to the Leaf Block Assembly Diagram, sew (1) 2¼" x 18½" (5.7cm x 47cm) White BG strip along the left side of Column 1 and (1) 2" x 18½" (5.1cm x 47cm) Dark Green strip along the right.

3. Join (1) each of Column 2 and Column 1. Sew (1) 2¼" x 18½" (5.7cm x 47cm) White BG strip to the right side of the unit. Make 6 Leaf blocks. Square to 18½" if needed.

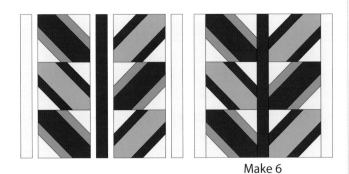

Make 6

Leaf Block Assembly Diagram

Finishing

1. Referring to the Quilt Assembly Diagram, join the blocks in rows of three, alternating the color of the Sunflower Blocks as shown. Join the rows.

2. Join (2) 3½" (8.9cm) x WOF White BG border strips end to end and press. Repeat to make (4) borders total. Sew the borders to the sides of the quilt top, trimming to fit, and press. Sew the remaining borders to the top and bottom of the quilt top, trimming to fit, and press.

Quilt Assembly Diagram

3. Layer the backing (wrong side up), batting, and quilt top (right side up); baste. Quilt as desired.

4. Bind the quilt.

Pumpkin Spice

Jack-o'-lanterns, crows, and giant pumpkins are all telltale signs that the spooky time of year has officially arrived! These four giant pumpkins make a delightful wall hanging to help usher in the season. You can also sew them side by side for a delightful Halloween-themed table runner.

Finished Size: 40" (101.6cm) square
Designed, pieced, and quilted by Sherilyn Mortensen
Quilt bound by Amy Maxfield
Fabric: Moda Grunge, stash

Fabric Requirements
- ⅓ yard (0.3m) each of Rust, Dark Orange, and Black
- 15" (38.1m) x Width of Fabric (WOF) Orange
- 15" (38.1m) x WOF Light orange
- ¼ yard (0.2m) Green fabric
- 1 yard (0.9m) White Background fabric
- 2¾ yards (2.5m) Backing fabric
- ⅓ yard (0.3m) Binding fabric

Cutting Instructions

From Rust fabric (bottom right Pumpkin block), cut:
- (2) 4½" (11.4cm) squares
- (4) 6½" (16.5cm) squares
- (2) 3½" x 6½" (8.9cm x 16.5cm) rectangles

From Dark Orange fabric (upper left Pumpkin block), cut:
- (2) 4½" (11.4cm) squares
- (4) 6½" (16.5cm) squares
- (2) 3½" x 6½" (8.9cm x 16.5cm) rectangles

From Orange fabric (Crow Pumpkin), cut:
- (5) 4½" (11.4cm) squares
- (1) 5" (12.7cm) square
- (2) 3½" (8.9cm) squares
- (1) 3½" x 6½" (8.9cm x 16.5cm) rectangle
- (1) 6½" x 9½" (16.5cm x 24.1cm) rectangle
- (1) 2" x 3½" (5.1cm x 8.9cm) rectangle

From Light Orange fabric (Jack-o'-lantern Pumpkin), cut:
- (3) 4½" (11.4cm) squares
- (1) 6½" (16.5cm) square
- (2) 3½" x 6½" (8.9cm x 16.5cm) rectangles
- (8) 3½" (8.9cm) squares
- (1) 1¼" x 12½" (3.2cm x 31.8cm) rectangle
- (3) 2" (5.1cm) squares

From Green fabric (Stems), cut:
- (8) 3" (7.6cm) squares
- (4) 2" x 6½" (5.1cm x 16.5cm) rectangles
- (8) 2" (5.1cm) squares

From Black fabric (Crows/Jack-o'-lantern), cut:
- (5) 4½" (11.4cm) squares
- (1) 5" (12.7cm) square
- (4) 2" (5.1cm) squares
- (2) 3½" (8.9cm) squares
- (2) 1¼" x 3½" (3.2cm x 8.9cm) rectangles
- (2) 2 x 2¾" (5.1cm x 7cm) rectangles
- (2) 2¾" (7cm) squares
- (3) 1¼" x 2" (3.2cm x 5.1cm) rectangles

From White Background fabric, cut:
- (8) 4½" (11.4cm) squares
- (8) 3" (7.6cm) squares
- (4) 3½" (8.9cm) squares
- (8) 5" x 6½" (12.7cm x 16.5cm) rectangles
- (8) 2" x 5" (5.1cm x 12.7cm) rectangles
- (8) 2" x 3½" (5.1cm x 8.9cm) rectangles
- (4) 2" (5.1cm) squares
- (4) 2½" (6.4cm) x width of fabric (WOF) border strips

Unit Assembly

Press seams as desired, taking care to nest the seams by pressing in either direction. Seams that don't need nesting can be pressed in either direction.

1. Following the Half Square Triangle (HST) instructions on page 8, make the following HST units from 4½" (11.4cm) squares. Press seams open and trim to 3½" (8.9cm) square.

- (4) Rust/White units from (2) squares each
- (4) Dark Orange/White units from (2) squares each
- (4) Orange/White units from (2) squares each
- (6) Orange/Black units from (3) squares each
- (4) Light Orange/White units from (2) squares each
- (2) Light Orange/Black units from (1) square each

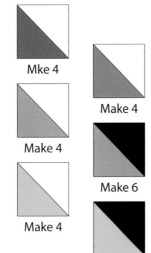

Mke 4

Make 4

Make 4

Make 6

Make 4

Make 2

2. Make (16) Green/White HST units from (8) 3" (7.6cm) squares each. Press the seams open and trim to 2" (5.1cm) square.

Make 16

3. Make (1) 4½" (11.4cm) Black/Orange HST unit from (1) 5" (12.7cm) square each Orange and Black, pressing the seams open. Do not square. Following the Quarter Half Square Triangle (QHST) instructions on page 9, join (1) 4½" (11.4cm) Orange/Black HST unit (not squared) and (1) 4½" (11.4cm) Black square. Press the seams open and trim to 3½" (8.9cm) square. Note: Be sure to use the correct QHST unit as shown. The remaining QHST and HST units will not be used.

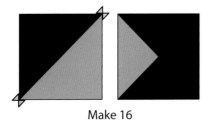

Make 16

4. Following the Corner Flip instructions on page 10, make the following CF units, pressing the seams open.
- (4) 3½" (8.9cm) White/Green CF units from (4) 3½" (8.9cm) White squares and (4) 2" (5.1cm) Green squares, joining (1) Green square onto a corner of each White square
- (4) 3½" (8.9cm) Light Orange/Black CF units from (4) 3½" (8.9cm) Light Orange squares and (4) 2" (5.1cm) Black squares, joining a Black square onto a corner of each Light Orange square

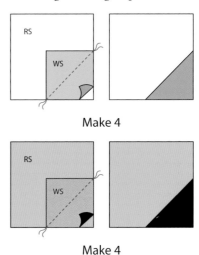

Make 4

Make 4

Block Assembly

Refer to the individual block diagrams throughout assembly. Stitch and press the seams as desired, taking care to nest seams by alternating pressing directions. Seams that don't need nesting can be pressed in either direction.

Pumpkin Stem Block

Block size: 6½" x 18½" (16.5cm x 47cm) (Make 4)
Assemble each block using:
- (2) 5" x 6½" (12.7cm x 16.5cm) White rectangles
- (2) 2" x 5" (5.1cm x 12.7cm) White rectangles
- (2) 2" x 3½" (5.1cm x 8.9cm) White rectangles
- (1) 2" (5.1cm) White square
- (1) 2" (5.1cm) Green square
- (1) 2" x 6½" (5.1cm x 16.5cm) Green rectangle
- (1) 3½" (8.9cm) White/Green CF unit
- (4) 2" (5.1cm) Green/White HST units

1. Referring to the Pumpkin Stem Assembly Diagram, join (1) 2" (5.1cm) square each White and Green. Sew (1) 3½" (8.9cm) White/Green CF unit to the top of the Green/White squares with the green fabric facing. Press the seams.

2. Join (2) 2" (5.1cm) Green/White HST units, sewing (1) 2" x 3½" (5.1cm x 8.9cm) White rectangle to the right side of the unit, then sew the other 2" x 3½" (5.1cm x 8.9cm) White rectangle to the top.

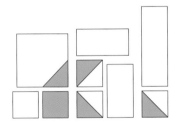

3. Join the units you just made. Sew (1) 2" x 6½" (5.1cm x 16.5cm) Green rectangle to the bottom of the units. Join (1) 2" (5.1cm) Green/White HST unit and (1) 2" x 5" (5.1cm x 12.7cm) White rectangle. Make (2) units.

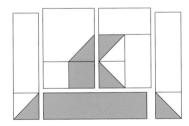

4. Sew (1) Green/White HST rectangle to either side of the Stem unit, then join (1) 5" x 6½" (12.7cm x 16.5cm) White rectangle to the right and left of the unit to complete the block. Make 4 blocks.

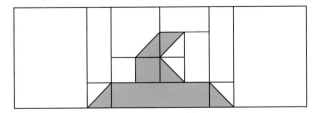

Pumpkin Stem Assembly Diagram

Pumpkin Block

Block size: 18½" (47cm) square (Make 2)
Assemble each block using:
- (1) 6½" x18½" (16.5cm x 47.9cm) Stem block
- (4) 3½" (8.9cm) Dark Orange/White (BG) HST units
- (2) 3½" x 6½" (8.9cm x 16.5cm) Dark Orange rectangles
- (4) 6½" (16.5cm) Dark Orange squares

1. Referring to the Dark Orange Pumpkin Block Assembly Diagram, sew (1) 3½" (8.9cm) Dark Orange/White (BG) HST unit to either end of (1) 3½" x 6½" (8.9cm x 16.5cm) Dark Orange rectangle. Make (2) units.

2. Join (4) 6½" (16.5cm) Dark Orange squares in a four patch. Sew (1) Dark Orange/White HST unit on either side of the center blocks as shown.

3. Sew (1) Stem Block to the top of the pumpkin unit to complete the Dark Orange Pumpkin block.

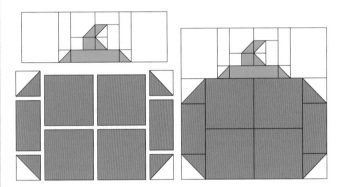

Dark Orange Pumpkin Block Assembly Diagram

4. In the same manner, make a Rust Pumpkin block using (1) 6½" x 18½" (16.5cm x 47.9cm) Stem block, (4) 3½" (8.9cm) Rust/White (BG) HST units, (2) 3½" x 6½" (8.9cm x 16.5cm) Rust rectangles, and (4) 6½" (16.5cm) Rust squares.

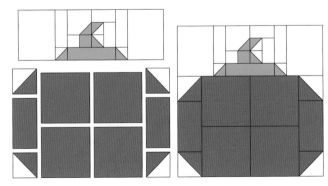

Rust Pumpkin Block Assembly Diagram

Crow Pumpkin Block

Block size: 18½" (47cm) square (Make 1)
Assemble the block using:
- (4) 3½" (8.9cm) Orange/White (BG) HST units
- (2) 3½" (8.9cm) Orange squares
- (1) 2" x 3½" (6.4cm x 8.9cm) Orange rectangle
- (1) 3½" x 6½" (8.9cm x 16.5cm) Orange rectangle
- (1) 6½" x 9½" (16.5cm x 24.1cm) Orange rectangle
- (6) 3½" (8.9cm) Orange/Black HST units
- (1) 3½" (8.9cm) Orange/Black/Black QHST unit
- (2) 3½" (8.9cm) Black squares
- (2) 1¼" x 3½" (3.2cm x 8.9cm) Black rectangles
- (1) 6½" x 18½" (16.5cm x 47cm) Pumpkin Stem block

1. Sew (1) 1¼" x 3½" (3.8cm x 8.9cm) Black rectangle to the left and right sides of (1) 2" x 3½" (6.4cm x 8.9cm) Orange rectangle for the leg unit. Square to 3½" (8.9cm), if necessary.

2. Referring to the Crow Pumpkin Block Assembly Diagram for placement and orientation of units, join the following 3½" (8.9cm) square units in rows of three, then join the rows.
Row 1: (1) 3½" (8.9cm) Orange/White (BG) HST unit and (2) 3½" (8.9cm) Orange/Black HST units
Row 2: (1) 3½" (8.9cm) Orange/Black HST unit, (1) 3½" (8.9cm) Orange/Black/Black QHST unit, and (1) 3½" (8.9cm) Black square
Row 3: (2) 3½" (8.9cm) Orange/Black HST units and (1) 3½" (8.9cm) Black square, alternating the units
Row 4: (1) 3½" (8.9cm) Orange/White (BG) HST unit, (1) 3½" (8.9cm) square leg unit, and (1) 3½" (8.9cm) Orange square

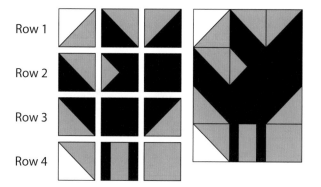

3. Join (1) 3½" (8.9cm) Orange/Black HST unit and (1) 3½" (8.9cm) Orange square. Sew (1) 6½" x 9½" (16.5cm x 24.1cm) Orange rectangle to the bottom of the unit.

4. Join (2) 3½" (8.9cm) Orange/White (BG) HST units on either end of (1) 3½" x 6½" (8.9cm x 16.5cm) Orange rectangle.

5. Join the sections. Sew (1) Pumpkin Stem unit along the top to complete the block.

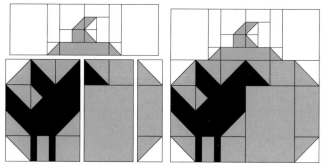

Crow Pumpkin Block Assembly Diagram

Jack-o'-lantern Block

Block size: 18½" (47cm) square (Make 1)
Assemble the block using:
- (2) 2¾" (7cm) Black squares
- (2) 2 x 2¾" (5.1cm x 7cm) Black rectangles
- (3) 1¼" x 2" (3.2cm x 5.1cm) Black rectangles
- (3) 2" (5.1cm) Light Orange squares
- (1) 1¼" x 12½" (3.2cm x 31.8cm) Light Orange rectangle
- (4) 3½" (8.9cm) Light Orange/White (BG) HST units
- (2) 3½" (8.9cm) Light Orange squares
- (2) 3½" x 6½" (8.9cm x 16.5cm) Light Orange rectangles
- (1) 6½" (16.5cm) Light Orange square
- (2) 3½" (8.9cm) Light Orange/Black HST units
- (4) 3½" (8.9cm) Light Orange/Black CF units
- (1) 6½" x 18½" (16.5cm x 47cm) Pumpkin Stem block

1. Referring to the Jack-o'-lantern Teeth Unit Assembly Diagram, join (1) 2" (5.1cm) Light Orange square and (1) 1¼" x 2" (3.2cm x 5.1cm) Black rectangle as shown; make 3 units. Referring to the diagram for placement, join the (3) Black/Light Orange rectangle units with (2) 2¾" (7cm) Black squares and (2) 2" x 2¾" (5.1cm x 7cm) Black rectangles. Sew (1) 1¼" x 12½" (3.2cm x 31.8cm) Light Orange rectangle along the bottom.

2. Following the Corner Flip (CF) instructions on page 10, join (1) 3½" (8.9cm) Light Orange square on the bottom left and right of the mouth section.

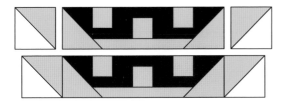

Jack-o-Lantern Teeth Unit Assembly Diagram

3. Sew (1) 3½" (8.9cm) Light Orange/White (BG) HST unit to either end of the unit to complete the mouth section.

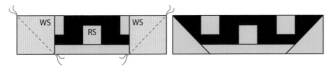

4. Join (1) 3½" (8.9cm) Light Orange/White (BG) HST unit and (1) 3½" x 6½" (8.9cm x 16.5cm) Light Orange rectangle. Join (1) 3½" (8.9cm) Light Orange/Black CF unit, (1) 3½" (8.9cm) Light Orange/Black HST unit, and (1) 3½" (8.9cm) Light Orange square as shown. Join the units with the Black/Orange unit on the right as show. Make a second unit with the Black/Orange unit on the left.

5. Join (2) 3½" (8.9cm) Light Orange/Black CF units with the black corners facing. Then sew (1) 6½" (16.5cm) Light Orange square to the top.

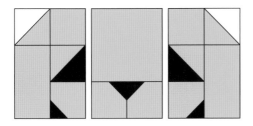

6. Referring to the diagram, join the 4 sections. Sew (1) Green Stem block to the top to complete the block.

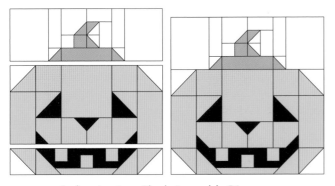

Jack-o-Lantern Block Assembly Diagram

Finishing the Quilt Top

1. Referring to the Quilt Assembly Diagram, join the blocks in rows of two, then join the rows.

2. Sew (1) 2½" (6.4cm) x (WOF) border strip to either side of the quilt top. Trim to fit and press. Sew (1) 2½" (6.4cm) x (WOF) border strip to the top and bottom of the quilt. Trim to fit and press.

Quilt Assembly Diagram

3. Layer the quilt top, batting, and batting; baste. Quilt as desired.

4. Bind the quilt.

Windy Days

Fall is a gorgeous time of year in Utah with vibrant trees, warm breezes, and the earthy fragrance of dried leaves on the ground. This beautiful wall hanging is made with nine Leaf blocks, all dressed in the vibrant and beautiful colors of fall.

Finished size: 40" (101.6cm) square
Designed, pieced, and quilted by Sherilyn Mortensen
Quilt bound by Amy Maxfield
Fabric: Mod Cloth by Sew Kind of Wonderful for Free Spirit

Fabric Requirements

- ⅛ yard (0.1m) each Red, Dark Red, Orange, Light Orange, Dark Green, Green, Light Green, Mint, Dark Purple, Purple, Light Purple, Pink, Dark Yellow, Gold, Yellow, and Light Yellow
- 4" x 8" (10.2cm x 20.3cm) rectangle each Peach, Light Mint, Light Pink, and Pale Yellow
- 4" x 18" (10.2cm x 45.8cm) rectangle each Dark brown, Brown, and Coral
- 4" x 13" (10.2cm x 33cm) Medium peach
- 3½" (8.9cm) square Light peach
- ¼ yard (0.2m) each Light gray, Dark gray, Medium gray, Gray, and Tan
- ⅓ yard (0.3m) Gray sashing for borders
- 2¾ yards (2.5m) Backing fabric
- ⅓ yard (0.3m) Binding fabric

Cutting Instructions

RED LEAF BLOCKS

From Dark Red fabric, cut:
- (4) 2½" (6.4cm) squares
- (2) 3½" (8.9cm) squares
- (4) 1" (2.5cm) squares

From Red fabric, cut:
- (2) 2½" (6.4cm) squares
- (4) 2½" x 4½" (6.4cm x 11.4cm) rectangles
- (2) 3½" (8.9cm) squares

From Orange fabric, cut:
- (2) 2½" (6.4cm) squares
- (4) 2½" x 4½" (6.4cm x 11.4cm) rectangles
- (2) 3½" (8.9cm) squares

From Light Orange fabric, cut:
- (6) 2½" (6.4cm) squares
- (2) 3½" (8.9cm) squares

From Peach fabric, cut:
- (2) 3½" (8.9cm) squares

From Light Gray fabric, cut:
- (2) 2½" (6.4cm) squares
- (10) 3½" (8.9cm) squares
- (4) 2½" x 10½" (6.4cm x 26.7cm) rectangles
- (8) 2" (5.1cm) squares

GREEN LEAF BLOCKS

From Dark Green fabric, cut:
- (4) 2½" (6.4cm) squares
- (2) 3½" (8.9cm) squares
- (4) 1" (2.5cm) squares

From Green fabric, cut:
- (2) 2½" (6.4cm) squares
- (4) 2½" x 4½" (6.4cm x 11.4cm) rectangles
- (2) 3½" (8.9cm) squares

From Light Green fabric, cut:
- (2) 2½" (6.4cm) squares
- (4) 2½" x 4½" (6.4cm x 11.4cm) rectangles
- (2) 3½" (8.9cm) squares

From Mint fabric, cut:
- (6) 2½" (6.4cm) squares
- (2) 3½" (8.9cm) squares

From Light Mint fabric, cut:
- (2) 3½" (8.9cm) squares

From Dark Gray fabric, cut:
- (2) 2½" (6.4cm) squares
- (10) 3½" (8.9cm) squares
- (4) 2½" x 10½" (6.4cm x 26.7cm) rectangles
- (8) 2" (5.1cm) squares

PURPLE LEAF BLOCKS

From Dark Purple fabric, cut:
- (4) 2½" (6.4cm) squares
- (2) 3½" (8.9cm) squares
- (4) 1" (2.5cm) squares

From Purple fabric, cut:
- (2) 2½" (6.4cm) squares
- (4) 2½" x 4½" (6.4cm x 11.4cm) rectangles
- (2) 3½" (8.9cm) squares

From Light Purple fabric, cut:
- (2) 2½" (6.4cm) squares
- (4) 2½" x 4½" (6.4cm x 11.4cm) rectangles
- (2) 3½" (8.9cm) squares

From Pink fabric, cut:
- (6) 2½" (6.4cm) squares
- (2) 3½" (8.9cm) squares

From Light Pink fabric, cut:
- (2) 3½" (8.9cm) squares

From Medium Gray fabric, cut:
- (2) 2½" (6.4cm) squares
- (10) 3½" (8.9cm) squares
- (4) 2½" x 10½" (6.4cm x 26.7cm) rectangles
- (8) 2" (5.1cm) squares

FOR YELLOW LEAF BLOCKS

From Dark Yellow fabric, cut:
- (4) 2½" (6.4cm) squares
- (2) 3½" (8.9cm) squares
- (4) 1" (2.5cm) squares

From Gold fabric, cut:
- (2) 2½" (6.4cm) squares
- (4) 2½" x 4½" (6.4cm x 11.4cm) rectangles
- (2) 3½" (8.9cm) squares

From Yellow fabric, cut:
- (2) 2½" (6.4cm) squares
- (4) 2½" x 4½" (6.4cm x 11.4cm) rectangles
- (2) 3½" (8.9cm) squares

From Light Yellow fabric, cut:
- (6) 2½" (6.4cm) squares
- (2) 3½" (8.9cm) squares

From Pale Yellow fabric, cut:
- (2) 3½" (8.9cm) squares

From Tan fabric, cut:
- (2) 2½" (6.4cm) squares
- (10) 3½" (8.9cm) squares
- (4) 2½" x 10½" (6.4cm x 26.7cm) rectangles
- (8) 2" (5.1cm) squares

FOR BROWN LEAF BLOCK

From Dark Brown fabric, cut:
- (2) 2½" (6.4cm) squares
- (1) 3½" (8.9cm) square
- (2) 1" (2.5cm) squares

From Brown fabric, cut:
- (1) 2½" (6.4cm) square
- (2) 2½" x 4½" (6.4cm x 11.4cm) rectangles
- (1) 3½" (8.9cm) square

From Coral fabric, cut:
- (1) 2½" (6.4cm) square
- (2) 2½" x 4½" (6.4cm x 11.4cm) rectangles
- (1) 3½" (8.9cm) square

From Medium Peach fabric, cut:
- (3) 2½" (6.4cm) squares
- (1) 3½" (8.9cm) square

From Light Peach fabric, cut:
- (1) 3½" (8.9cm) square

From Gray fabric, cut:
- (1) 2½" (6.4cm) square
- (5) 3½" (8.9cm) squares
- (2) 2½" x 10½" (6.4cm x 26.7cm) rectangles
- (4) 2" (5.1cm) squares
- (4) 2½" (6.4cm) x Width of fabric (WOF) strips for the borders

Assembly

1. Following the Half Square Triangle (HST) instructions on page 8, use the 3½" (8.9cm) squares to make the following HST units, pressing the seams open and trimming to 2½" (6.4cm) square:

For Red Leaf Blocks
- (4) Dark Red/Light Gray units from (2) squares each
- (4) Red/Light Gray units from (2) squares each
- (4) Orange/Light Gray units from (2) squares each
- (4) Light Orange/Light Gray units from (2) squares each
- (4) Peach/Light Gray units from (2) squares each

Make 4 of Each

For Green Leaf Blocks

- (4) Dark Green/Dark Gray units from (2) squares each
- (4) Green/Dark Gray units from (2) squares each
- (4) Light Green/Dark Gray units from (2) squares each
- (4) Mint/Dark Gray units from (2) squares each
- (4) Light Mint/Dark Gray units from (2) squares each

    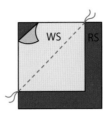

Make 4 of Each

For Purple Leaf Blocks

- (4) Dark Purple/Medium Gray units from (2) squares each
- (4) Purple/Medium Gray units from (2) squares each
- (4) Light Purple/Medium Gray units from (2) squares each
- (4) Pink/Medium Gray units from (2) squares each
- (4) Light Pink/Medium Gray units from (2) squares each

Make 4 of Each

For Yellow Leaf Blocks

- (4) Dark Yellow/Tan units from (2) squares each
- (4) Gold/Tan units from (2) squares each
- (4) Yellow/Tan units from (2) squares each
- (4) Light Yellow/Tan units from (2) squares each
- (4) Pale Yellow/Tan units from (2) squares each

Make 4 of Each

For Brown Leaf Block

- (2) Dark Brown/Gray units from (1) square each
- (2) Brown/Gray units from (1) square each
- (2) Coral/Gray units from (1) square each
- (2) Medium Peach/Gray units from (1) square each
- (2) Light Peach/Gray units from (1) square each

Make 2 of Each

2. Following the Corner Flip (CF) directions on page 10, make the following CF units, sewing the 2" (5.1cm) squares onto opposite corners of the 2½" (6.4cm) squares. Press seams open.

- (4) 2½" (6.4cm) Dark Red/Light Gray CF units from (4) 2½" (6.4cm) Dark Red squares and (8) 2" (5.1cm) Light Gray squares for the Red Leaf Blocks

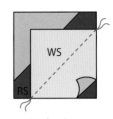 

Make 4

- (4) 2½" (6.4cm) Dark Green/Dark Gray CF units from (4) 2½" (6.4cm) Dark Green squares and (8) 2" (5.1cm) Dark Gray squares for the Green Leaf Blocks
- (4) 2½" (6.4cm) Dark Purple/Medium Gray CF units from (4) 2½" (6.4cm) Dark Purple squares and (8) 2" (5.1cm) Medium Gray squares for the Purple Leaf Blocks
- (4) 2½" (6.4cm) Dark Yellow/Tan CF units from (4) 2½" (6.4cm) Dark Yellow squares and (8) 2" (5.1cm) Tan squares for the Yellow Leaf Blocks
- (2) 2½" (6.4cm) Dark Brown/Gray CF units from (2) 2½" (6.4cm) Dark Brown squares and (4) 2" (5.1cm) Gray squares for the Brown Leaf Block

Make 4 of Each   Make 2

3. Following the (CF) directions on page 10, make the following CF units, sewing half of the 1" (2.5cm) squares in each color combination onto the upper left corner of the 2½" x 10½" (6.4cm x 26.7cm) rectangles and the other half onto the right as shown.

- (4) 2½" x 10½" (6.4cm x 26.7cm) Light Gray/ Dark Red CF units from (4) 2½" x 10½" (6.4cm x 26.7cm) Light Gray vertical rectangles and (4) 1" (2.5cm) Dark Red squares for the Red Leaf Block

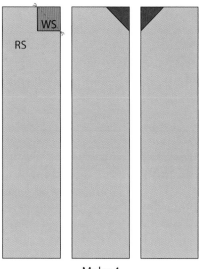

Make 4

- (4) 2½" x 10½" (6.4cm x 26.7cm) Dark Gray/ Dark Green CF units from (4) 2½" x 10½" (6.4cm x 26.7cm) Dark Gray rectangles and (4) 1" (2.5cm) Dark Green squares for the Green Leaf Block
- (4) 2½" x 10½" (6.4cm x 26.7cm) Medium Gray/Dark Purple CF units from (4) 2½" x 10½" (6.4cm x 26.7cm) Medium Gray rectangles and (4) 1" (2.5cm) Dark Purple squares for the Purple Leaf Block

Make 4 of Each

- (4) 2½" x 10½" (6.4cm x 26.7cm) Tan/Dark Yellow CF units from (4) 2½" x 10½" (6.4cm x 26.7cm) Tan rectangles and (4) 1" (2.5cm) Dark Yellow squares for the Yellow Leaf Blocks
- (2) 2½" x 10½" (6.4cm x 26.7cm) Gray/Dark Brown CF units from (2) 2½" x 10½" (6.4cm x 26.7cm) Gray rectangles and (2) 1" (2.5cm) Dark Brown squares for the Brown Leaf Blocks

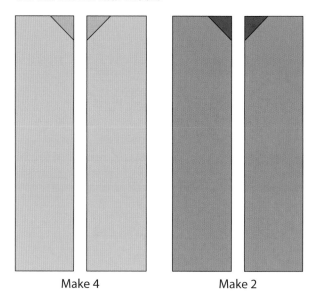

Make 4   Make 2

Leaf Block Assembly

Block size: 12½" (31.8cm) square
Note: All of the Leaf Blocks are assembled in the same manner. Press the seams, taking care to nest the seams by alternating pressing directions. Seams that don't need nesting can be pressed in either direction.

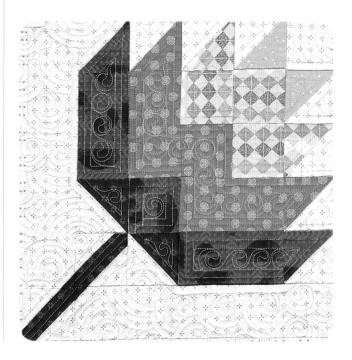

RED LEAF BLOCK (MAKE 2)

Refer to the Leaf Block Assembly Diagram throughout assembly. Lay out the units as shown, then join them in sections as follows.

Each Red Leaf Block uses:
- (2) 2½" (6.4cm) Dark Red/Light Gray HST units
- (2) 2½" (6.4cm) Red/Light Gray HST units
- (2) 2½" (6.4cm) Orange/Light Gray HST units
- (2) 2½" (6.4cm) Light Orange/Light Gray HST units
- (2) 2½" (6.4cm) Peach/Light Gray HST units
- (1) 2½" (6.4cm) Red square
- (1) 2½" (6.4cm) Orange square
- (3) 2½" (6.4cm) Light Orange squares
- (1) 2½" (6.4cm) Light Gray square
- (2) 2½" x 4½" (6.4cm x 11.4cm) Red rectangles
- (2) 2½" x 4½" (6.4cm x 11.4cm) Orange rectangles
- (2) 2½" (6.4cm) Dark Red/Light Gray CF units
- (2) 2½" x 10½" (6.4cm x 26.7cm) Light Gray/Dark Red CF units

1. Section 1: Join (1) 2½" (6.4cm) Red/Light Gray HST unit and (1) 2½" x 4½" (6.4cm x 11.4cm) Red rectangle. Join (1) 2½" (6.4cm) Orange/Light Gray HST unit and (1) 2½" x 4½" (6.4cm x 11.4cm) Orange rectangle. Sew the units together with the Red/Gray unit on the left. Make a second unit with the Red/Gray unit on the right, noting the orientation of the HST units and the finished unit.

2. Section 2: Join the following 2½" (6.4cm) square units in rows, then join the rows and press.
Row 1: (1) Light Orange/Light Gray HST unit, (1) Peach/Light Gray HST unit, and (1) Light Gray square
Row 2: (2) Light Orange squares and (1) Peach/Light Gray HST unit, noting the direction of the HST unit
Row 3: (1) Orange square, (1) Light Orange square, and (1) Light Orange/Light Gray HST unit, noting the direction of the HST units

3. Section 3: Join (2) 2½" (6.4cm) Dark Red/Light Gray HST units, (1) 2½" (6.4cm) Red square, and (1) 2½" (6.4cm) Dark Red/Light Gray CF unit to form a four patch unit. Press.

4. Join the sections you just made in rows, then join the rows. Sew (1) 2½" x 10½" (6.4cm x 26.7cm) Light Gray/ Dark Red CF unit to the bottom of the block center. Join (1) 2½" (6.4cm) Dark Red/Light Gray CF unit and (1) 2½" x 10½" (6.4cm x 26.7cm) Light Gray/Dark Red CF unit. Sew the unit to the left side of the unit to complete the block. Make 2 Red Leaf Blocks.

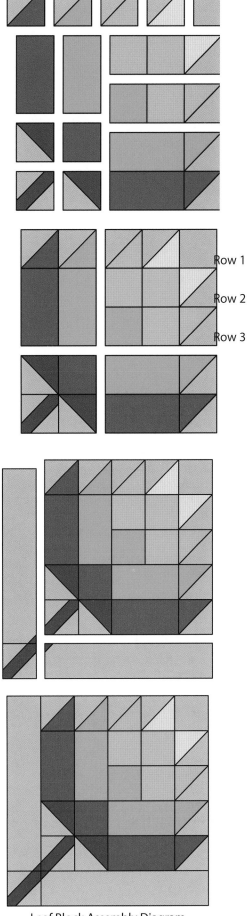

Leaf Block Assembly Diagram

5. Assemble the remaining blocks in the same manner.

GREEN LEAF BLOCK (MAKE 2)

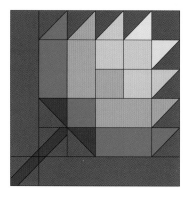

Each block uses:
- (2) 2½" (6.4cm) Dark Green/Dark Gray HST units
- (2) 2½" (6.4cm) Green/Dark Gray HST units
- (2) 2½" (6.4cm) Light Green/Dark Gray HST units
- (2) 2½" (6.4cm) Mint/Dark Gray HST units
- (2) 2½" (6.4cm) Light Mint/Dark Gray HST units
- (1) 2½" (6.4cm) Green square
- (1) 2½" (6.4cm) Light Green square
- (3) 2½" (6.4cm) Mint squares
- (1) 2½" (6.4cm) Dark Gray square
- (2) 2½" x 4½" (6.4cm x 11.4cm) Green rectangles
- (2) 2½" x 4½" (6.4cm x 11.4cm) Light green rectangles
- (2) 2½" (6.4cm) Dark Green/Dark Gray CF units
- (2) 2½" x 10½" (6.4cm x 26.7cm) Dark Gray/Dark Green CF units as shown

PURPLE LEAF BLOCK (MAKE 2)

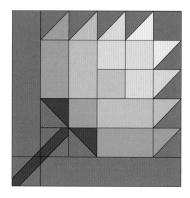

Each block uses:
- (2) 2½" (6.4cm) Dark Purple/Medium Gray HST units
- (2) 2½" (6.4cm) Purple/Medium Gray HST units
- (2) 2½" (6.4cm) Light Purple/Medium Gray HST units
- (2) 2½" (6.4cm) Pink/Medium Gray HST units
- (2) 2½" (6.4cm) Light Pink/Medium Gray HST units
- (1) 2½" (6.4cm) Purple square
- (1) 2½" (6.4cm) Light Purple square
- (3) 2½" (6.4cm) Pink squares

- (1) 2½" (6.4cm) Medium Gray square
- (2) 2½" x 4½" (6.4cm x 11.4cm) Purple rectangles
- (2) 2½" x 4½" (6.4cm x 11.4cm) Light Purple rectangles
- (2) 2½" (6.4cm) Dark Purple/Medium Gray CF units
- (2) 2½" x 10½" (6.4cm x 26.7cm) Medium Gray/Dark Purple CF units as shown

YELLOW LEAF BLOCK (MAKE 2)

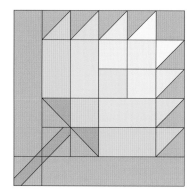

Each block uses:
- (2) 2½" (6.4cm) Dark Yellow/Tan HST units
- (2) 2½" (6.4cm) Gold/Tan HST units
- (2) 2½" (6.4cm) Yellow/Tan HST units
- (2) 2½" (6.4cm) Light Yellow/Tan HST units
- (2) 2½" (6.4cm) Pale Yellow/Tan HST units
- (1) 2½" (6.4cm) Gold square
- (1) 2½" (6.4cm) Yellow square
- (3) 2½" (6.4cm) Light Yellow squares
- (1) 2½" (6.4cm) Tan square
- (2) 2½" x 4½" (6.4cm x 11.4cm) Gold rectangles
- (2) 2½" x 4½" (6.4cm x 11.4cm) Yellow rectangles
- (2) 2½" (6.4cm) Dark Yellow/Tan CF units
- (2) 2½" x 10½" (6.4cm x 26.7cm) Tan/Dark Yellow CF units as shown

BROWN LEAF BLOCK (MAKE 1)

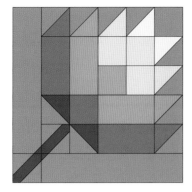

The block uses:
- (2) 2½" (6.4cm) Dark Brown/Gray HST units
- (2) 2½" (6.4cm) Brown/Gray HST units
- (2) 2½" (6.4cm) Coral/Gray HST units
- (2) 2½" (6.4cm) Medium Peach/Gray HST units
- (2) 2½" (6.4cm) Light Peach/Gray HST units
- (1) 2½" (6.4cm) Brown square
- (1) 2½" (6.4cm) Coral square
- (3) 2½" (6.4cm) Medium Peach squares
- (1) 2½" (6.4cm) Gray square
- (2) 2½" x 4½" (6.4cm x 11.4cm) Brown rectangles
- (2) 2½" x 4½" (6.4cm x 11.4cm) Coral rectangles
- (2) 2½" (6.4cm) Dark Brown/Gray CF units
- (2) 2½" x 10½" (6.4cm x 26.7cm) Gray/Dark Brown CF units as shown

Finishing the Quilt Top

1. Referring to the Quilt Block Assembly Diagram, join the Leaf blocks in rows of three, alternating the colors. Join the rows and press.

2. Sew (1) 2½" (6.4cm) x WOF Gray border strip to either side of the quilt top. Trim to fit and press. Sew the remaining 2½" (6.4cm) x WOF Gray borders to the top and bottom. Trim to fit and press.

3. Layer the backing, batting, and quilt top; baste. Quilt as desired.

4. Bind the quilt.

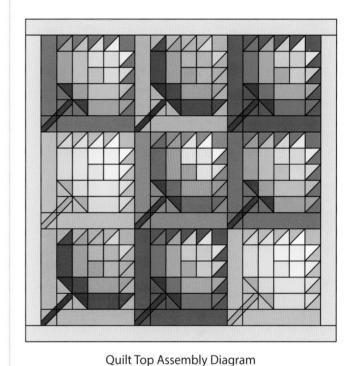

Quilt Top Assembly Diagram

Apple Crisp

Apples in all their colors and forms are one of life's most delicious delectables! This three-block quilt is a beautiful representation of this beloved fall fruit. It makes a festive fall runner, or you can create more blocks to turn the design into a seasonally themed throw or wall hanging.

18" x 54" (45.7cm x 137.2cm)
Designed, pieced, and quilted by: Sherilyn Mortensen
Fabric: Mod Cloth by Sew Kind of Wonderful for
  Free Spirit

Fabric Requirements

- ¼ yard (0.2m) each of Yellow, Red, and Green
- ⅓ yard (0.3m) each of Beige, Tan, and Cream
- 3" (7.6cm) square each of Light Yellow, Pink, and Light green
- 4" (10.2cm) x Width of Fabric (WOF) or 10" (25.4Cm) square Dark green
- 2" x 12" (5.1cm x 30.5cm) rectangle of Brown
- 2½ yards (2.3m) Backing fabric
- ⅓ yard (0.3m) Binding fabric

Cutting Instructions

YELLOW APPLE

From Yellow fabric, cut:
- (1) 2¾" x 6½" (7cm x 16.5cm) rectangle
- (2) 2" (5.1cm) squares
- (1) 6½" x 8¾" (16.5cm x 22.2cm) rectangle
- (1) 3½" x 6½" (8.9cm x 16.5cm) rectangle
- (1) 3" (7.6cm) square
- (1) 4½" (11.4cm) square

From Light Yellow fabric, cut:
- (1) 3" (7.6cm) square

From Beige fabric, cut:
- (3) 2" (5.1cm) squares
- (1) 2" x 3½" (5.1cm x 8.9cm) rectangle
- (1) 2¾" x 3½" (7cm x 8.9cm) rectangle
- (1) 3½" (8.9cm) square
- (3) 3" (7.6cm) squares
- (1) 4½" (11.4cm) square
- (2) 3½" x 12½" (8.9cm x 31.8cm) rectangles
- (2) 3½" x 18½" (8.9cm x 47cm) rectangles

From Brown fabric (stems), cut:
- (3) 1¼" x 3½" (3.2cm x 8.9cm) rectangles

From Dark Green fabric (leaves), cut:
- (9) 3" (7.6cm) squares

RED APPLE

From Red fabric, cut:
- (1) 2¾" x 6½" (7cm x 16.5cm) rectangle
- (2) 2" (5.1cm) squares
- (1) 6½" x 8¾" (16.5cm x 22.2cm) rectangle
- (1) 3½" x 6½" (8.9cm x 16.5cm) rectangle
- (1) 3" (7.6cm) square
- (1) 4½" (11.4cm) square

From Pink fabric, cut:
- (1) 3" (7.6cm) square

From Tan fabric, cut:
- (3) 2" (5.1cm) squares
- (1) 2 x 3½" (5.1cm x 8.9cm) rectangle
- (1) 2¾" x 3½" (7cm x 8.9cm) rectangle
- (1) 3½" (8.9cm) square
- (3) 3" (7.6cm) squares
- (1) 4½" (11.4cm) square
- (2) 3½" x 12½" (8.9cm x 31.8cm) rectangles
- (2) 3½" x 18½" (8.9cm x 47cm) rectangles

GREEN APPLE

From Green fabric, cut:
- (1) 2¾" x 6½" (7cm x 16.5cm) rectangle
- (2) 2" (5.1cm) squares
- (1) 6½" x 8¾" (16.5cm x 22.2cm) rectangle
- (1) 3½" x 6½" (8.9cm x 16.5cm) rectangle
- (1) 3" (7.6cm) square
- (1) 4½" (11.4cm) square

From Light Green fabric, cut:
- (1) 3" (7.6cm) square

From Cream fabric, cut:
- (3) 2" (5.1cm) squares
- (1) 2 x 3½" (5.1cm x 8.9cm) rectangle
- (1) 2¾" x 3½" (7cm x 8.9cm) rectangle
- (1) 3½" (8.9cm) square
- (3) 3" (7.6cm) squares
- (1) 4½" (11.4cm) square
- (2) 3½" x 12½" (8.9cm x 31.8cm) rectangles
- (2) 3½" x 18½" (8.9cm x 47cm) rectangles

Assembly

1. Following the Half-Square Triangle (HST) instructions on page 8, make the following HST units from (1) 4½" (11.4cm) square each of Yellow, Beige, Red, Tan, Green, and Cream to create (2) HST units each in Yellow/Beige, Red/Tan, and Green/Cream. Press and trim to 3½" (8.9cm) square.

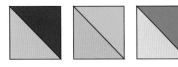

Make 2 of Each

2. In the same manner, make the following HST units from 3" (7.6cm) squares. Press and trim to 2" (5.4cm) square. Note: Some HST units will not be used.
- (2) Yellow/Light Yellow units from (1) square each
- (2) Red/Pink units from (1) square each
- (2) Green/Light Green units from (1) square each
- (5) Dark Green/Beige units from (3) squares each
- (5) Dark Green/Tan units from (3) squares each
- (5) Dark Green/Cream units from (3) squares each

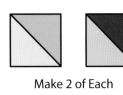

Make 2 of Each

Make 5 of Each

3. Following the Corner Flip (CF) instructions on page 10, make the following CF units, sewing (1) 2" (5.1cm) square to the upper left corner of a 2¾" x 6½" (7.1cm x 16.5cm) vertical rectangle. Press the seams open. Make CF units in the following combinations:
- (1) Yellow/Beige CF unit from (1) Yellow rectangle and (1) Beige square
- (1) Red/Tan CF unit from (1) Red rectangle and (1) Tan square
- (1) Green/Cream CF unit from (1) Green rectangle and (1) Cream square

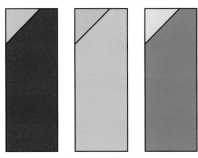

Make 1 of Each

4. In the same manner, make the following CF units, sewing a 2" (5.1cm) square to the upper right corner of a 6½" x 8¾" (16.5cm x 22.2cm) horizontal rectangle. Press the seams open.
- (1) Yellow/Beige CF unit from (1) Yellow horizontal rectangle and (1) Beige square
- (1) Red/Tan CF Unit from (1) Red horizontal rectangle and (1) Tan square
- (1) Green/Cream CF unit from (1) Green horizonal rectangle and (1) Cream square

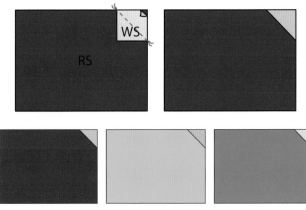

Make 1 of Each

Apple Block Assembly

Block size: 18½" (47cm) square
All of the blocks are assembled in the same manner. Be sure to note the orientation of the HST and CF units when assembling each row. Stitch and press seams as desired, taking care to nest the seams by alternating the pressing directions. Seams that don't need nesting can be pressed in either direction.

Assemble (1) Red Apple Block using the following pieces:
- (5) 2" (5.1cm) Dark Green/Tan HST units
- (2) 3½" (8.9cm) Red/Tan HST units
- (2) 2" (5.1cm) Red/Pink HST units
- (1) 2¾" x 6½" (7cm x 16.5cm) Red/Tan CF unit
- (1) 6½" x 8¾" (16.5cm x 22.2cm) Red/Tan CF unit
- (1) 3½" x 6½" (8.9cm x 16.5cm) Red Rectangle
- (2) 2" (5.1cm) Red Squares
- (1) 1¼" x 3½" (3.2cm x 8.9cm) Brown rectangle
- (1) 2" (5.1cm) Tan square
- (1) 2" x 3½" (5.1cm x 8.9cm) Tan rectangle
- (1) 2¾" x 3½" (7cm x 8.9cm) Tan rectangle
- (1) 3½" (8.9cm) Tan square
- (2) 3½" x 12½" (8.9cm x 31.8cm) Tan rectangles
- (2) 3½" x 18½" (8.9cm x 47cm) Tan rectangles

1. Referring to the Row 1 Assembly Diagram for orientation and placement, join (2) 2" (5.1cm) Dark Green/Tan HST units. Sew (1) 2" x 3½" (5.1cm x 8.9cm) Tan horizontal rectangle along the top and (1) 2¾" x 3½" (7cm x 8.9cm) Tan vertical rectangle to the left side. For the right side, join (1) 2" (5.1cm) Tan square and (3) 2" (5.1cm) Dark Green/Tan HST units in a four patch. Then sew (1) 3½" (8.9cm) tan square to the right side. Sew (1) HST unit to either side of the 1¼" x 3½" (3.2cm x 8.9cm) Brown rectangle as shown to complete Row 1.

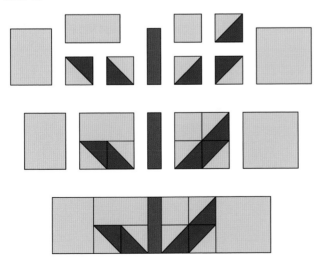

Row 1 Assembly Diagram

2. Referring to the Row 2 Assembly Diagram, join (2) 2" (5.1cm) Red Squares and (2) 2" (5.1cm) Red/Pink HST units in a column, alternating the direction of the HST units as shown. Sew (1) 2¾" x 6½" (7cm x 16.5cm) Red/Tan CF unit to the left side of the HST unit and (1) 6½" x 8¾" (16.5cm x 22.2cm) Red/Tan CF unit to the right to complete Row 2.

Row 2 Assembly Diagram

3. Sew (1) 3½" (8.9cm) Red/Tan HST unit to either end of the 3½" x 6½" (8.9cm x 16.5cm) Red Rectangle to complete Row 3.

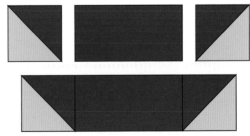

Row 3 Assembly Diagram

4. Join the rows as shown.

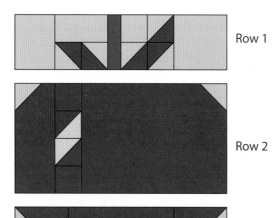

Row 1

Row 2

Row 3

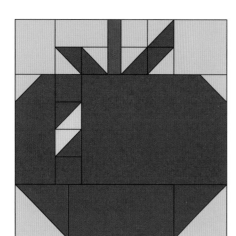

Center Apple

5. Sew (1) 3½" x 12½" (8.9cm x 31.8cm) Tan rectangle to either side of the Apple unit. Then sew (1) 3½" x 18½" (8.9cm x 47cm) Tan rectangle to the top and bottom to complete the Red Apple Block.

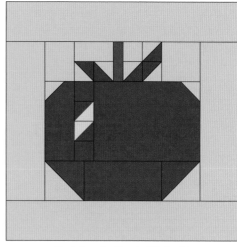

Red Apple Block (Make 1)

6. In the same manner, make the Yellow and Green Apple blocks.

Assemble (1) Yellow Apple Block using:
- (5) 2" (5.1cm) Dark Green/Beige HST units
- (2) 3½" (8.9cm) Yellow/Beige HST units
- (2) 2" (5.1cm) Yellow/Light Yellow HST Units
- (1) 2¾" x 6½" (7cm x 16.5cm) Yellow/Beige CF Unit
- (1) 6½" x 8¾" (16.5cm x 22.2cm) Yellow/Beige CF unit
- (1) 3½" x 6½" (8.9cm x 16.5cm) Yellow rectangle
- (2) 2" (5.1cm) Yellow squares
- (1) 1¼" x 3½" (3.2cm x 8.9cm) brown rectangle
- (1) 2" (5.1cm) Beige square
- (1) 2" x 3½" (5.1cm x 8.9cm) Beige rectangle
- (1) 2¾" x 3½" (7cm x 8.9cm) Beige rectangle
- (1) 3½" (8.9cm) Beige square
- (2) 3½" x 12½" (8.9cm x 31.8cm) Beige rectangles
- (2) 3½" x 18½" (8.9cm x 47cm) Beige rectangles

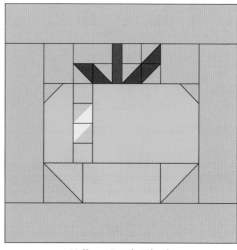

Yellow Apple Block

Assemble (1) Green Apple Block:

- (5) 2" (5.1cm) Dark Green/Cream HST units
- (2) 3½" (8.9cm) Green/Cream HST units
- (2) 2" (5.1cm) Green/Light Green HST units
- (1) 2¾" x 6½" (7cm x 16.5cm) Green/Cream CF unit
- (1) 6½" x 8¾" (16.5cm x 22.2cm) Green/Cream CF unit
- (1) 3½" x 6½" (8.9cm x 16.5cm) Green rectangle
- (2) 2" (5.1cm) Green squares
- (1) 1¼" x 3½" (3.2cm x 8.9cm) Brown rectangle
- (1) 2" (5.1cm) Cream square
- (1) 2" x 3½" (5.1cm x 8.9cm) Cream rectangle
- (1) 2¾" x 3½" (7cm x 8.9cm) Cream rectangle
- (1) 3½" (8.9cm) Cream square
- (2) 3½" x 12½" (8.9cm x 31.8cm) Cream rectangles
- (2) 3½" x 18½" (8.9cm x 47cm) Cream rectangles

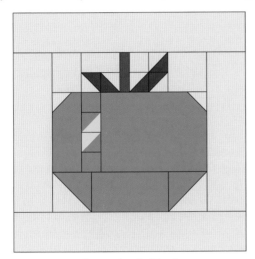

Green Apple Block

Finishing the Runner

1. Join the Red, Yellow, and Green Apple Blocks as shown.

2. Layer the backing, batting, and quilt top; baste. Quilt as desired.

3. Bind the quilt.

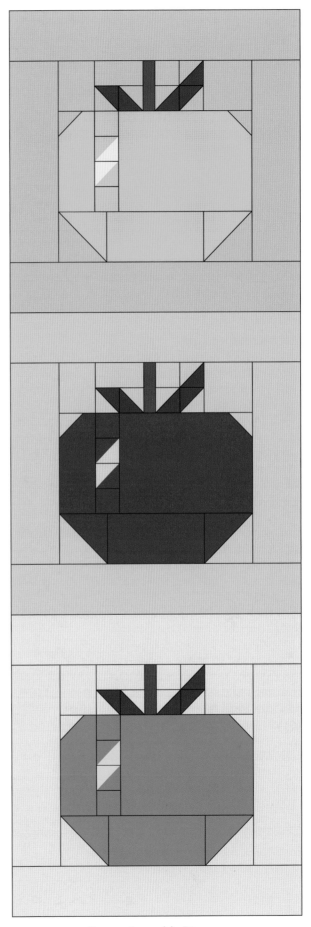

Runner Assembly Diagram

Frosty's Family

Growing up on Utah's beautiful Wasatch front, our winter landscape always included a blanket of fresh white snow sprinkled with children's footprints, snow angels and, of course, a snowman! This generous-size throw is made up of 12 colorful snowmen, each boasting a playful variation on the same design.

54" x 72" (137.2cm x 182.9cm)
Designed and quilted by Sherilyn Mortensen
Pieced and bound by Amy Maxfield
Fabric: Kaufman Essex, V and Co. Ombre Confetti, Moda Grunge

Fabric Requirements
- 3" (7.6cm) x WOF or (1) 10" square each of Dark Purple, Purple, Light Purple, Green, Light Green, Orange, Aqua, Mint, Light Blue, Pink, and Light Pink
- ¼ yard (0.2m) Black
- 1 yard (0.9m) White
- 3¼ yards (3m) Dark Blue background (BG) fabric
- 4 yards (3.7m) Backing fabric
- ½ yard (0.5m) Binding fabric

Cutting Instructions:

From each of the Dark Purple, Lime Green, Orange, and Light Blue fabrics (scarves), cut:
- (6) 2" x 3½" (5.1cm x 8.9cm) rectangles
- (3) 2" x 6½" (5.1cm x 16.5cm) rectangles

From each of the Purple, Green, Aqua, and Pink fabrics (top/bottom of hat), cut:
- (3) 1¼" x 2" (3.2cm x 5.1cm) rectangles
- (3) 2" x 6½" (5.1cm x 16.5cm) rectangles

From each of the Light Purple, Light Green, Mint, and Light Pink fabrics (hat middle), cut:
- (3) 2" x 6½" (5.1cm x 16.5cm) rectangles

From White fabric (snowmen bodies), cut:
- (24) 1¼" (3.2cm) squares
- (60) 2" (5.1cm) squares
- (72) 2" x 3½" (5.1cm x 8.9cm) rectangles
- (24) 3½" x 6½" (8.9cm x 16.5cm) rectangles

From Black fabric (eyes/buttons), cut:
- (168) 1¼" (3.2cm) squares

From Dark Blue Background fabric, cut:
- (12) 2" x 2¾" (5.1cm x 7cm) rectangles
- (72) 2" (5.1cm) squares
- (24) 3½" x 5¾" (8.9cm x 14.6cm) rectangles
- (12) 3½" x 5" (8.9cm x 12.7cm) rectangles
- (12) 3½" x 6½" (8.9cm x 16.5cm) rectangles
- (12) 3½" x 12½" (8.9cm x 31.8cm) rectangles
- (24) 3½" x 18½" (8.9cm x 47.6cm) rectangles

Assembly

1. Following the Corner Flip (CF) instructions on page 10, make (3) 2" x 6½" (5.1cm x 16.5cm) CF units each in Light Purple/Dark Blue (BG), Light Green/Dark Blue (BG), Light Pink/Dark Blue (BG), and Mint/Dark Blue (BG) using (3) 2" x 6½" (5.1cm x 16.5cm) rectangles each in Light Purple, Light Green, Light Pink, and Mint and (6) 2" (5.1cm) Dark Blue (BG) per color combination, sewing (1) square to the top right and left corners of each horizontal rectangle. Press the seams open.

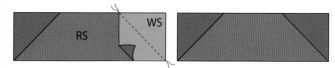

Make 3

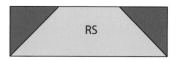

Make 3

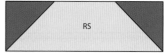

Make 3

Make 3

2. In the same manner as above, make (24) 3½" x 6½" (8.9cm x 16.5cm) White/Dark Blue (BG) CF units from (24) 3½" x 6½" (8.9cm x 16.5cm) White horizontal rectangles and (48) 2" (5.1cm) Dark Blue (BG) squares.

Make 24

3. Make (24) 2" (5.1cm) White/Black CF units from (24) 2" (5.1cm) White squares and (36) 1¼" (3.2cm) Black squares, sewing (1) Black square on the lower left corner of (12) White squares and (2) Black squares on the same side of (12) White squares as shown, sewing the Black squares on the corners and corner flipping the units one at a time (they are supposed to overlap).

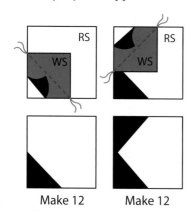

Make 12   Make 12

4. Make the following 2" x 3½" (5.1cm x 8.9cm) CF units from (72) 2" x 3½" (5.1cm x 8.9cm) White rectangles and (108) 1¼" (3.2cm) Black squares in the following combinations:

- Sew (1) Black Square on the bottom right corner of (24) White rectangles
- Sew (1) Black square on the top right corner of (12) White rectangles
- Sew (2) Black squares on the top and bottom left of (36) White rectangles, sewing the black squares on the corners and corner flipping the units one at a time (they are supposed to overlap)

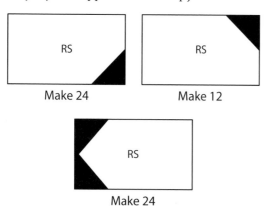

Make 24   Make 12

Make 24

Snowman Blocks

Block size: 18½" (47cm) square

All of the Snowman Blocks are made in the same manner. Make (3) Snowman Blocks in each color combination: Purple Scarf/Green Hat, Light Blue Scarf/Pink Hat, Orange Scarf/Aqua Hat, Light Blue scarf/Purple Hat, and Lime Green Scarf/Pink Hat. When pressing, take care to nest the seams by alternating pressing directions. Seams that don't need nesting can be pressed in either direction.

Each Purple Scarf/Green Hat Snowman requires:

- (1) 2" x 6½" (5.1cm x 16.5cm) Light Green/Dark Blue (BG) CF unit
- (2) 3½" x 6½" (8.9cm x 16.5cm) White/Dark Blue (BG) CF units
- (2) 2" (5.1cm) White/Black CF units (as shown for buttons)
- (6) 2" x 3½" (5.1cm x 8.9cm) White/Black CF units (as shown for buttons)
- (1) 1¼" x 2" (3.2cm x 5.1cm) Green rectangle
- (1) 2" x 6½" (5.1cm x 16.5cm) Green rectangle
- (2) 2" x 3½" (5.1cm x 8.9cm) Dark Purple rectangles
- (1) 2" x 6½" (5.1cm x 16.5cm) Dark Purple rectangle
- (3) 2" (5.1cm) White squares
- (2) 1¼" (3.2cm) White squares
- (2) 1¼" (3.2cm) Black squares
- (1) 2" x 2¾" (5.1cm x 7cm) Dark Blue (BG) rectangle
- (1) 3½" x 5" (8.9cm x 12.7cm) Dark Blue (BG) rectangle
- (1) 3½" x 6½" (8.9cm x 16.5cm) Dark Blue (BG) rectangle
- (2) 3½" x 5¾" (8.9cm x 14.6cm) Dark Blue (BG) rectangles
- (1) 3½" x 12½" (8.9cm x 31.8cm) Dark Blue (BG) rectangle
- (2) 3½" x 18½" (8.9cm x 47.6cm) Dark Blue (BG) rectangles

1. Referring to the Snowman Hat diagram, join (1) 1¼" x 2" (3.2cm x 5.1cm) Green rectangle and (1) 2" x 2¾" (5.1cm x 7cm) Dark Blue (BG) rectangle. Sew (1) 3½" x 5¾" (8.9cm x 14.6cm) Dark Blue (BG) rectangle on either side of the Green/Dark Blue (BG) unit.

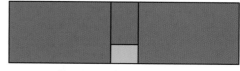

Snowman Hat Diagram

2. Join (1) 1¼" (3.2cm) square each White and Black. Make (2) White/Black units. Join the White/Black units with (3) 2" (5.1cm) White squares in a row, alternating the units as shown. Sew (1) 2" x 6½" (5.1cm x 16.5cm Dark Purple rectangle to the bottom of the White/Black unit and (1) 2" x 6½" (5.1cm x 16.5cm) Green rectangle to the top, then join (1) 2" x 6½" (5.1cm x 16.5cm) Light Green/Dark Blue (BG) CF unit to the top of the unit. Join (1) 2" x 3½" (5.1cm x 8.9cm) Dark Purple rectangle and (1) 5" x 3½" (5.1cm x 8.9cm) Dark Blue rectangle. Sew the Dark Purple/Dark Blue unit to the right side of the White/Black unit. Sew (1) 3½" x 6½" (8.9cm x 16.5cm) Dark Blue (BG) rectangle to the left side to complete the block.

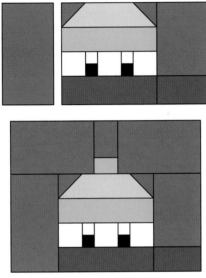

Snowman Hat Diagram

3. Referring to the Snowman Body Diagram, join (4) 2" x 3½" (5.1cm x 8.9cm) White/Black CF units with the black "buttons" pointing to the right. Sew (1) 3½" x 6½" (8.9cm x 16.5cm) White/Dark Blue (BG) CF unit to the left side as shown. Then join (2) 2" x 3½" (5.1cm x 8.9cm) White/Black CF units with the "buttons" pointing to the left. Set the unit aside. Join (2) 2" (5.1cm) White/Black CF units. Sew the White/Black CF units to the left side of (1) 2" x 3½" (5.1cm x 8.9cm) Dark Purple rectangle. Join the Black/White button units as shown. Sew (1) 3½" x 6½" (8.9cm x 16.5cm) White/Dark Blue (BG) CF unit to the right side to complete the section.

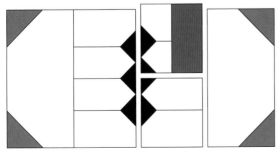

Snowman Body Diagram

4. Referring to the Snowman Block Assembly Diagram, join the units as shown. Sew (1) 3½" x 12½" (8.9cm x 31.8cm) Dark Blue (BG) rectangle along the bottom. Then sew (1) 3½" x 18½" (8.9cm x 47.6cm) Dark Blue (BG) rectangle to either side of the snowman to complete the block. Make 3 blocks.

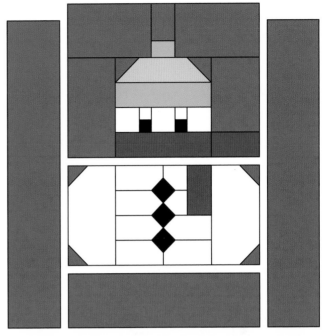

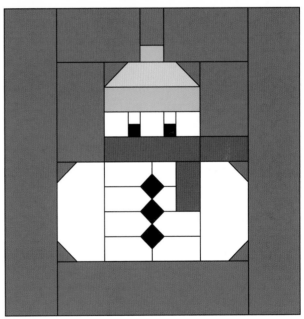

Snowman Block Assembly Diagram
Make 3 Purple Scarf/Green Hat

5. Make (3) 18½" (47cm) square Snowman Blocks each in Orange Scarf/Aqua Hat, Light Blue Scarf/Purple Hat Snowman, Lime Green Scarf/Pink Hat, Dark Purple Scarf/Green Hat.

Orange Scarf/Aqua Hat

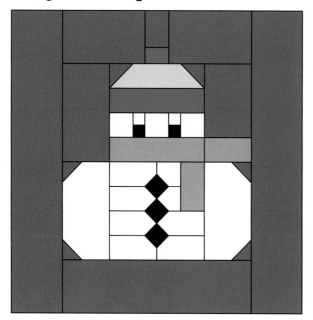

Make 3

Each block uses:

- (1) 2" x 6½" (5.1cm x 16.5cm) Mint/Dark Blue (BG) CF unit
- (2) 3½" x 6½" (8.9cm x 16.5cm) White/Dark Blue (BG) CF units
- (2) 2" (5.1cm) White/Black CF units (as shown for buttons)
- (6) 2" x 3½" (5.1cm x 8.9cm) White/Black CF units (as shown for buttons)
- (1) 1¼" x 2" (3.2cm x 5.1cm) Aqua rectangle
- (1) 2" x 6½" (5.1cm x 16.5cm) Aqua rectangle
- (2) 2" x 3½" (5.1cm x 8.9cm) Orange rectangles
- (1) 2" x 6½" (5.1cm x 16.5cm) Orange rectangle
- (3) 2" (5.1cm) White squares
- (2) 1¼" (3.2cm) White squares
- (2) 1¼" (3.2cm) Black squares
- (1) 2" x 2¾" (5.1cm x 7cm) Dark Blue (BG) rectangle
- (1) 3½" x 5" (8.9cm x 12.7cm) Dark Blue (BG) rectangle
- (1) 3½" x 6½" (8.9cm x 16.5cm) Dark Blue (BG) rectangle
- (2) 3½" x 5¾" (8.9cm x 14.6cm) Dark Blue (BG) rectangles
- (1) 3½" x 12½" (8.9cm x 31.8cm) Dark Blue (BG) rectangle
- (2) 3½" x 18½" (8.9cm x 47.6cm) Dark Blue (BG) rectangles

Light Blue Scarf/Purple Hat

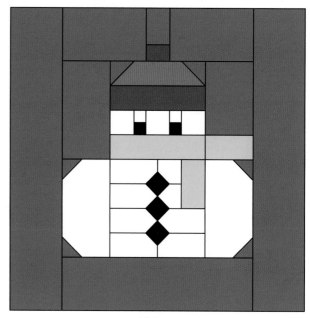

Make 3

Each block uses:

- (1) 2" x 6½" (5.1cm x 16.5cm) Light Purple/Dark Blue (BG) CF unit
- (2) 3½" x 6½" (8.9cm x 16.5cm) White/Dark Blue (BG) CF units
- (2) 2" (5.1cm) White/Black CF units (as shown for buttons)
- (6) 2" x 3½" (5.1cm x 8.9cm) White/Black CF units (as shown for buttons)
- (1) 1¼" x 2" (3.2cm x 5.1cm) Purple rectangle
- (1) 2" x 6½" (5.1cm x 16.5cm) Purple rectangle
- (2) 2" x 3½" (5.1cm x 8.9cm) Light Blue rectangles
- (1) 2" x 6½" (5.1cm x 16.5cm) Light Blue rectangle
- (3) 2" (5.1cm) White squares
- (2) 1¼" (3.2cm) White squares
- (2) 1¼" (3.2cm) Black squares
- (1) 2" x 2¾" (5.1cm x 7cm) Dark Blue (BG) rectangle
- (1) 3½" x 5" (8.9cm x 12.7cm) Dark Blue (BG) rectangle
- (1) 3½" x 6½" (8.9cm x 16.5cm) Dark Blue (BG) rectangle
- (2) 3½" x 5¾" (8.9cm x 14.6cm) Dark Blue (BG) rectangles
- (1) 3½" x 12½" (8.9cm x 31.8cm) Dark Blue (BG) rectangle
- (2) 3½" x 18½" (8.9cm x 47.6cm) Dark Blue (BG) rectangles

Lime Green Scarf/Pink Hat

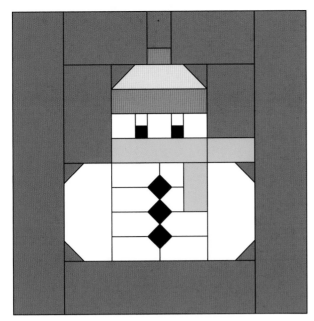

Make 3

Each block uses:

- (1) 2" x 6½" (5.1cm x 16.5cm) Light Pink/Dark Blue (BG) CF unit
- (2) 3½" x 6½" (8.9cm x 16.5cm) White/Dark Blue (BG) CF units
- (2) 2" (5.1cm) White/Black CF units (as shown for buttons)
- (6) 2" x 3½" (5.1cm x 8.9cm) White/Black CF units (as shown for buttons)
- (1) 1¼" x 2" (3.2cm x 5.1cm) Pink rectangle
- (1) 2" x 6½" (5.1cm x 16.5cm) Pink rectangle
- (2) 2" x 3½" (5.1cm x 8.9cm) Lime Green rectangles
- (1) 2" x 6½" (5.1cm x 16.5cm) Lime Green rectangle
- (3) 2" (5.1cm) White squares
- (2) 1¼" (3.2cm) White squares
- (2) 1¼" (3.2cm) Black squares
- (1) 2" x 2¾" (5.1cm x 7cm) Dark Blue (BG) rectangle
- (1) 3½" x 5" (8.9cm x 12.7cm) Dark Blue (BG) rectangle
- (1) 3½" x 6½" (8.9cm x 16.5cm) Dark Blue (BG) rectangle
- (2) 3½" x 5¾" (8.9cm x 14.6cm) Dark Blue (BG) rectangles
- (1) 3½" x 12½" (6.4cm x 31.8cm) Dark Blue (BG) rectangle
- (2) 3½" x 18½" (8.9cm x 47.6cm) Dark Blue (BG) rectangles

Finishing the Quilt Top

1. Join the blocks in rows of three, alternating the colors of the Hat/Scarves as shown. Join the rows.

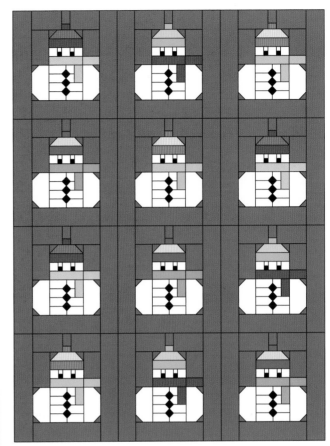

Quilt Assembly Diagram

2. Layer the quilt top, batting, and backing; baste. Quilt as desired.

3. Bind the quilt.

Snow Day

I have wonderful memories of my young children playing in the snow, all bundled up with rosy cheeks and giant grins. This nine-block quilt reminds me of those Snow Days—no school, no work, just plenty of fresh snow to make an awesome snowman. It is the perfect size for a fun winter wall hanging.

36" x 38" (91.4cm x 96.5cm)
Designed, pieced, and quilted by Sherilyn Mortensen
Quilt bound by Amy Maxfield
Fabric: Moda Grunge, stash

Fabric Requirements
- ⅓ yard (0.3m) White
- 3" (7.6cm) x Width of Fabric (WOF) or (1) 10" (25.4cm) square Peach
- 3" (7.6cm) x WOF each Green, Yellow, and Black
- ¼ yard (0.2m) Red
- 7" (17.8cm) x WOF each Maroon and Blue
- 1½ yards (1.4m) Light Blue Background fabric
- 2⅔ yards (2.4m) Backing fabric
- 15" (38.1cm) x WOF Binding

Cutting Instructions

From White fabric (snowman body), cut:
- (2) 3½" (8.9cm) squares
- (3) 2½" (6.4cm) squares
- (3) 2½" x 4½" (6.4cm x 11.4cm) rectangles
- (5) 1½" (3.9cm) squares
- (1) 2½" x 6½" (6.4cm x 16.5cm) rectangle
- (1) 4½" x 8½" (11.4cm x 21.6cm) rectangle
- (1) 2½" x 3½" (6.4cm x 8.9cm) rectangle
- (1) 1½" x 2½" (3.9cm x 6.4cm) rectangle
- (1) 3½" x 8½" (8.9cm x 21.6cm) rectangle
- (1) 3½" x 5" (8.9cm x 12.7cm) rectangle
- (1) 3" x 3½" (7.6cm x 8.9cm) rectangle
- (1) 4½" x 7" (11.4cm x 17.8cm) rectangle
- (1) 3" x 4½" (7.6cm x 11.4cm) rectangle

From Blue fabric (hats/gloves), cut:
- (5) 3½" (8.9cm) squares
- (6) 2½" (6.4cm) squares
- (1) 4½" x 6½" (11.4cm x 16.5cm) rectangle

From Peach fabric (face), cut:
- (3) 2½" (6.4cm) squares
- (2) 1½" (3.9cm) squares

From Green fabric (scarf/fringe), cut:
- (4) 1" x 2½" (2.5cm x 6.4cm) rectangles
- (2) 2½" x 4½" (6.4cm x 11.4cm) rectangles
- (1) 2½" x 6½" (6.4cm x 16.5cm) rectangle

From Yellow fabric (hat rims/buttons/fringe), cut:
- (4) 1½" (3.9cm) squares
- (8) 1" x 2½" (2.5cm x 6.4cm) rectangles
- (2) 2½" (6.4cm) squares
- (1) 2½" x 6½" (6.4cm x 16.5cm) rectangle
- (1) 2½" x 8½" (6.4cm x 21.6cm) rectangle

From Red fabric (snowsuit), cut:
- (1) 3½" (8.9cm) square
- (4) 1½" (3.9cm) squares
- (2) 2½" x 6½" (6.4cm x 16.5cm) rectangles
- (2) 2½" x 4½" (6.4cm x 11.4cm) rectangles
- (1) 2½" (6.4cm) square
- (1) 4½" x 6½" (11.4m x 16.5cm) rectangle
- (1) 2½" x 4" (6.4cm x 10.2cm) rectangle
- (1) 2" x 2½" (5.1cm x 6.4cm) rectangle
- (1) 2" x 6½" (5.1cm x 16.5cm) rectangle
- (1) 4" x 6½" (10.2cm x 16.5cm) rectangle

From Maroon fabric (scarf/fringe), cut:
- (3) 3½" (8.9cm) squares
- (4) 1" x 2½" (2.5cm x 6.4cm) rectangles
- (2) 2½" (6.4cm) squares
- (2) 2½" x 4½" (6.4cm x 11.4cm) rectangles
- (1) 2½" x 8½" (6.4cm x 21.6cm) rectangle
- (1) 2½" x 6½" (6.4cm x 16.5cm) rectangle

From Black fabric (buttons/eyes/boots), cut:
- (8) 1½" (3.9cm) squares
- (1) 2½" (6.4cm) square
- (1) 2½" x 6½" (6.4cm x 16.5cm) rectangle

From Light Blue Background (BG) fabric, cut:
- (11) 3½" (8.9cm) squares
- (7) 2½" (6.4cm) squares
- (6) 2½" x 4½" (6.4cm x 11.4cm) rectangles
- (2) 2½" x 6½" (6.4cm x 16.5cm) rectangles
- (1) 2½" x 8½" (6.4cm x 21.6cm) rectangle
- (1) 2½" x 12½" (6.4cm x 31.8cm) rectangle
- (3) 4½" x 8½" (11.4cm x 21.6cm) rectangles
- (2) 4½" x 6½" (11.4cm x 16.5cm) rectangles
- (3) 6½" (16.5cm) squares
- (5) 4½" x 12½" (11.4cm x 31.8cm) rectangles
- (1) 6½" x 12½" (16.5cm x 31.8cm) rectangle
- (1) 2½" (6.4cm) x WOF strip for borders

Assembly

1. Following the Half Square Triangles (HST) instructions on page 8, make the following HST units from 3½" (8.9cm) squares. Press the seams open and trim each HST unit to 2½" (6.4cm) square.
- (10) Blue/Light Blue BG units from (5) squares each
- (4) White/Light Blue BG units from (2) squares each
- (5) Maroon/Light Blue BG units from (3) squares each (one HST will not be used)
- (2) Red/Light Blue BG units from (1) square each

| Make 10 | Make 4 | Make 5 | Make 2 |

Block Assembly

Size: 12½" (31.8cm)
Refer to the individual Block Unit Assembly Diagrams throughout assembly. When pressing, take care to nest the seams by alternating the pressing directions. Seams that don't need nesting can be pressed in either direction.

BLOCK A
Make (1) Block A using:
- (4) 2½" (6.4cm) Blue/Light Blue BG HST units
- (3) 2½" (6.4cm) Blue squares
- (1) 4½" x 6½" (11.4cm x 16.5cm) Blue rectangle
- (1) 2½" (6.4cm) Light Blue BG square
- (1) 2½" x 4½" (6.4cm x 11.4cm) Light Blue BG rectangle
- (1) 4½" x 8½" (11.4cm x 21.6cm) Light Blue BG rectangle
- (1) 4½" x 12½" (11.4cm x 31.8cm) Light Blue BG rectangle

1. Referring to the Block A Assembly Diagram, join (1) 2½" (6.4cm) Blue and (1) 2½" (6.4cm) Blue/Light Blue BG HST unit, then sew (1) 4½" x 6½" (11.4cm x 16.5cm) Blue rectangle to the right side.

2. Join the following units in rows, noting the orientation of the HST units:
Row 1: (1) 2½" (6.4cm) Light Blue BG square, (1) 2½" (6.4cm) Blue/Light Blue BG HST, and (1) 2½" (6.4cm) Blue square
Row 2: (1) 2½" (6.4cm) Blue/Light Blue BG HST, (1) 2½" (6.4cm) Blue square, (1) 2½" (6.4cm) Blue/Light Blue BG HST
Join the rows, then sew (1) 2½" x 4½" (6.4cm x 11.4cm) Light Blue BG vertical rectangle to the left side of the unit.

3. Join the units you just made. Sew (1) 4½" x 8½" (11.4cm x 21.6cm) Light Blue BG rectangle to the left side of the unit and (1) 4½" x 12½" (11.4cm x 31.8cm) Light Blue BG rectangle to the top to complete the block.

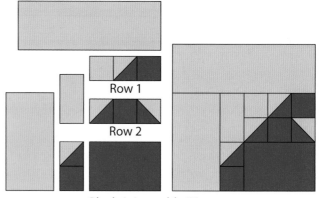

Block A Assembly Diagram

BLOCK B
Make (1) Block B using:
- (4) 2½" (6.4cm) Blue/Light Blue BG HST units
- (3) 2½" (6.4cm) Maroon/Light Blue BG HST units
- (1) 2½" (6.4cm) Blue square
- (1) 2½" (6.4cm) Yellow square
- (3) 2½" (6.4cm) Light Blue BG squares
- (2) 2½" x 4½" (6.4cm x 11.4cm) Light Blue BG rectangles
- (1) 4½" x 8½" (11.4cm x 21.6cm) Light Blue BG rectangle
- (1) 4½" x 12½" (11.4cm x 31.8cm) Light Blue BG rectangle

1. Referring to the Block B Assembly Diagram, join the following units in columns:
Column 1: (1) 2½" (6.4cm) Blue square and (3) 2½" (6.4cm) Blue/Light Blue BG HST units
Column 2: (1) 2½" (6.4cm) Light Blue square, (1) 2½" (6.4cm) Blue/Light Blue BG HST unit, and (1) 2½" x 4½" (6.4cm x 11.4cm) Light Blue BG rectangle
Column 3: (1) 2½" (6.4cm) Light Blue BG square, (1) 2½" (6.4cm) Maroon/Light Blue BG HST unit, and (1) 2½" x 4½" (6.4cm x 11.4cm) Light Blue BG rectangle
Column 4: (1) 2½" (6.4cm) Yellow square, (2) 2½" (6.4cm) Maroon/Light Blue BG HST units, and (1) 2½" (6.4cm) Light Blue BG square

2. Join columns 1 and 2, then join columns 3 and 4. Sew (1) column to either side of (1) 4½" x 8½" (11.4cm x 21.6cm) Light Blue BG rectangle as shown. Then sew (1) 4½" x 12½" (11.4cm x 31.8cm) Light Blue BG rectangle along the top to complete the block.

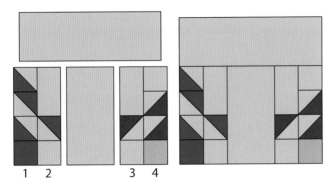

Block B Assembly Diagram

BLOCK C
Make (1) Block C using:
- (2) 2½" (6.4cm) Maroon/Light Blue BG HST units
- (1) 2½" (6.4cm) Maroon square
- (1) 2½" x 4½" (6.4cm x 11.4cm) Maroon rectangle
- (1) 2½" x 6½" (6.4cm x 16.5cm) Yellow rectangle
- (1) 2½" (6.4cm) Light Blue BG square
- (1) 6½" (16.5cm) Light Blue BG square
- (1) 6½" x 12½" (16.5cm x 31.8cm) Light Blue BG rectangle

1. Referring to the Block C Assembly Diagram, join (2) 2½" (6.4cm) Maroon/Light Blue BG HST units and (1) 2½" (6.4cm) square each of Maroon and Light Blue BG in a four patch. Sew (1) 2½" x 4½" (6.4cm x 11.4cm) Maroon rectangle to the left of the four patch unit. Then sew (1) 2½" x 6½" (6.4cm x 16.5cm) Yellow rectangle to the bottom.

2. Sew (1) 6½" (16.5cm) Light Blue BG square to the right side of the unit, then sew (1) 6½" x 12½" (16.5cm x 31.8cm) Light Blue BG rectangle to the top to complete the block.

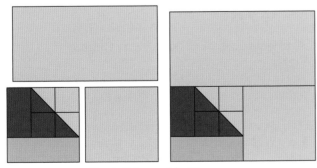

Block C Assembly Diagram

BLOCK D
Make (1) Block D using:
- (1) 2½" (6.4cm) White/Light Blue BG HST unit
- (1) 2½" (6.4cm) White square
- (1) 2½" x 4½" (6.4cm x 11.4cm) White rectangle
- (3) 1½" (3.9cm) White squares
- (1) 3" x 3½" (7.6cm x 8.9cm) White rectangle (right of buttons)
- (1) 3½" x 5" (8.9cm x 12.7cm) White rectangle (left of buttons)
- (1) 3½" x 8½" (8.9cm x 21.6cm) White rectangle (top of buttons)
- (1) 1½" x 2½" (3.9cm x 6.4cm) White rectangle
- (1) 2½" x 3½" (6.4cm x 8.9cm) White rectangle
- (4) 1½" (3.9cm) Black squares
- (1) 2½" x 8½" (6.4cm x 21.6cm) Maroon rectangle
- (1) 2½" x 8½" (6.4cm x 21.6cm) Yellow rectangle
- (1) 2½" x 6½" (6.4cm x 16.5cm) Light Blue BG rectangle
- (1) 2½" x 12½" (6.4cm x 31.8cm) Light Blue rectangle

1. To make the eye unit, join (1) 1½" (3.9cm) square each of Black and White to make the eye columns. (Square to 1½" x 2½" [3.8cm x 6.4cm].) Make 2 units. Referring to the Block H Assembly Diagram for placement, join the (2) eye units with (1) 2½" x 3½" (6.4cm x 8.9cm) White rectangle, (1) 2½" (6.4cm) White square, and (1) 1½" x 2½" (3.9cm x 6.4cm) White rectangle. Sew (1) 2½" x 8½" (6.4cm x 21.6cm) Maroon rectangle along the bottom and (1) 2½" x 8½" (6.4cm x 21.6cm) Yellow rectangle along the top. Sew (1) 2½" x 6½" (6.4cm x 16.5cm) vertical Light Blue BG rectangle to the left side.

2. To make the button unit, join (2) 1½" (3.9cm) Black squares and (1) 1½" (3.8cm) White square, alternating the colors, to form the "button column." (Square to 1½" x 3½" [3.8cm x 8.9cm].) Sew (1) 3½" x 5" (8.9cm x 12.7cm) White rectangle to the left side, (1) 3" x 3½" (7.6cm x 8.9cm) White rectangle to the right, and (1) 3½" x 8½" (8.9cm x 21.6cm) White rectangle along the top. Join (1) 2½" x 4½" (6.4cm x 11.4cm) White rectangle and (1) 2½" (6.4cm) White/Light Blue BG HST unit, then sew to the left side of the unit.

3. Join the Eye unit and Button unit as shown. Sew (1) 2½" x 12½" (6.4cm x 31.8) Light Blue BG rectangle to the left side to complete the block.

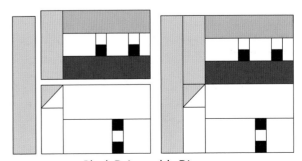

Block D Assembly Diagram

BLOCK E

Make (1) E block using:
- (1) 2½" (6.4cm) White/Light Blue BG HST unit
- (1) 2½" (6.4cm) Red/Light Blue BG HST unit
- (1) 2½" (6.4cm) White square
- (1) 2½" x 4½" (6.4cm x 11.4cm) White rectangle
- (1) 2½" (6.4cm) Yellow square
- (1) 2½" x 4½" (6.4cm x 11.4cm) Maroon rectangle
- (1) 2½" x 6½" (6.4cm x 16.5cm) Maroon rectangle
- (2) 1" x 2½" (2.5cm x 6.4cm) Maroon rectangles
- (6) 1" x 2½" (2.5cm x 6.4cm) Yellow rectangles
- (4) 1" x 2½" (2.5cm x 6.4cm) Green rectangles
- (2) 2½" x 4½" (6.4cm x 11.4cm) Green rectangles
- (1) 2½" (6.4cm) Red square
- (1) 2½" x 4½" (6.4cm x 11.4cm) Red rectangle
- (1) 2½" (6.4cm) Blue square
- (1) 2½" (6.4cm) Peach square
- (2) 2½" (6.4cm) Light Blue BG squares
- (1) 2½" x 4½" (6.4cm x 11.4cm) Light Blue BG rectangle
- (1) 2½" x 6½" (6.4cm x 16.5cm) Light Blue BG rectangle
- (1) 4½" x 6½" (11.4cm x 16.5cm) Light Blue BG rectangle

1. Referring to the Block E Assembly Diagram, join (1) 2½" (6.4cm) square each Yellow and White. Sew (1) 2½" x 4½" (6.4cm x 11.4cm) Light Blue BG rectangle to the right side and (1) 2½" x 4½" (6.4cm x 11.4cm) Maroon rectangle to the bottom. Then join (1) 2½" x 4½" (6.4cm x 11.4cm) White rectangle and (1) 2½" (6.4cm) White/Light Blue HST unit. Sew (1) 2½" x 6½" (6.4cm x 16.5cm) Maroon rectangle to the left side. Join the units you just made.

3. Join (2) 1" x 2½" (2.5cm x 6.4cm) rectangles each of Maroon and Yellow, alternating the colors to make a strip set. In the same manner, make (2) strip sets with (2) 1" x 2½" (2.5cm x 6.4cm) rectangles each Yellow and Green. (Trim the "fringe" units to 2½" [6.4cm] square.)

4. Sew (1) 2½" (6.4cm) Light Blue BG square to the left side of (1) 2½" (6.4cm) Yellow/Green strip set and (1) 2½" x 4½" (6.4cm x 11.4cm) Green rectangle to the right. Join (1) 2½" x 6½" (6.4cm x 16.5cm) Light Blue BG rectangle and (1) 2½" (6.4cm) Peach square. Join the units you just made.

5. Referring to the diagram, join (1) 2½" (6.4cm) Maroon/Yellow Fringe unit and (1) 2½" (6.4cm) Light Blue BG square. Sew (1) 4½" x 6½" (11.4cm x 16.5cm) Light Blue BG rectangle to the bottom as shown.

4. Join the following units in columns, then join the columns.
Column 1: (1) 2½" (6.4cm) Blue square, (1) 2½" x 4½" (6.4cm x 11.4cm) Red rectangle, and (1) 2½" (6.4cm) Red/Light Blue BG HST unit
Column 2: (1) 2½" (6.4cm) Red square, (1) 2½" (6.4cm) Yellow/Green Fringe unit, and (1) 2½" x 4½" (6.4cm x 11.4cm) Green rectangle

5. Join the sections to complete the block.

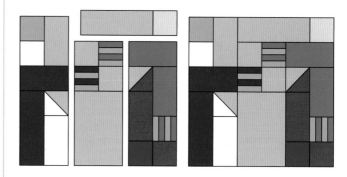

Block E Assembly Diagram

BLOCK F

Assemble (1) F block using:
- (1) 2½" (6.4cm) Red/Light Blue BG HST unit
- (1) 2½" x 4½" (6.4cm x 11.4cm) Red rectangle
- (1) 2½" x 6½" (6.4cm x 16.5cm) Red rectangle
- (1) 4" x 6½" (10.2cm x 16.5cm) Red rectangle (right of buttons)
- (1) 2" x 6½" (5.1cm x 16.5cm) Red rectangle (left of buttons)
- (3) 1½" (3.9cm) Red squares
- (3) 1½" (3.9cm) Yellow squares
- (1) 2½" (6.4cm) Blue square
- (1) 2½" x 6½" (6.4cm x 16.5cm) Green rectangle
- (2) 1½" (3.9cm) Black squares
- (2) 1½" (3.9cm) Peach squares
- (2) 2½" (6.4cm) Peach squares
- (1) 4½" x 6½" (11.4cm x 16.5cm) Light Blue BG rectangle
- (1) 4½" x 8½" (11.4cm x 21.6cm) Light Blue BG rectangle

1. Referring to the Block F Assembly Diagram for placement and orientation, join (3) 1½" (3.9cm) squares each of Yellow and Red to make the Button Column unit. Square to 1½" x 6½" (3.8cm x 16.5cm).

2. Join (1) 1½" (3.9cm) square each of Peach and Black as shown. Make 2 Eye Column units. Square to 1½" x 2½" (3.9cm x 6.4cm). Join the Eye Column units with (2) 2½" (6.4cm) Peach squares, alternating the placement as shown.

3. Sew (1) 2" x 6½" (5.1cm x 16.5cm) Red rectangle to the left side of the Button unit, (1) 4" x 6½" (10.2cm x 16.5cm) Red rectangle to the right, and (1) 2½" x 6½" (6.4cm x 16.5cm) Red rectangle to the top. Sew (1) 2½" x 6½" (6.4cm x 16.5cm) Green rectangle along the top, then join the Eye Column unit as shown.

4. Join (1) 2½" (6.4cm) Blue square, (1) 2½" x 4½" (6.4cm x 11.4cm) Red rectangle, and (1) Red/Light Blue BG HST unit. Sew (1) 4½" x 8½" (11.4cm x 21.6cm) Light Blue BG rectangle to the right side of the unit, then join (1) 4½" x 6½" (11.4cm x 16.5cm) Light Blue BG rectangle to the top of the unit.

5. Join the units as shown to complete the block.

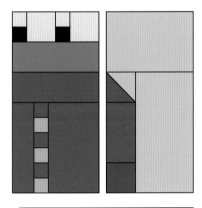

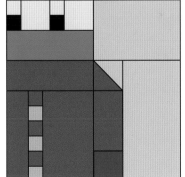

Block F Assembly Diagram

BLOCK G

Make (1) G block using:
- (1) 2½" (6.4cm) White/Light Blue BG HST unit
- (1) 2½" (6.4cm) White square
- (1) 4½" x 7" (11.4cm x 17.8cm) White rectangle (left of buttons)
- (1) 4½" x 8½" (11.4cm x 21.6cm) White rectangle
- (1) 3" x 4½" (7.6cm x 11.4cm) White rectangle (right of buttons)
- (2) 1½" (3.9cm) White squares
- (2) 1½" (3.9cm) Black squares
- (1) 2½" x 8½" (6.4cm x 21.6cm) Light Blue BG rectangle
- (1) 4½" x 12½" (11.4cm x 31.8cm) Light Blue BG rectangle

1. Referring to the Block G Assembly Diagram for placement, join (2) 1½" (3.9cm) squares each Black and White to create the Button Column unit. Square to 1½" x 4½" (3.8cm x 11.6cm). Sew (1) 4½" x 7" (11.4cm x 17.8cm) White rectangle to the left of the Button Column unit and (1) 3" x 4½" (7.6cm x 11.4cm) White rectangle to the right.

2. Join (1) 2½" (6.4cm) White/Light Blue BG HST unit and (1) 2½" (6.4cm) White square. Sew (1) 4½" x 8½" (11.4cm x 21.6cm) White rectangle to the right side of the unit.

3. Referring to the diagram, join the units you just made. Sew (1) 2½" x 8½" (6.4cm x 21.6cm) Light Blue BG rectangle to the left side. Sew (1) 4½" x 12½" (11.4cm x 31.8cm) Light Blue BG rectangle to the bottom to complete the unit.

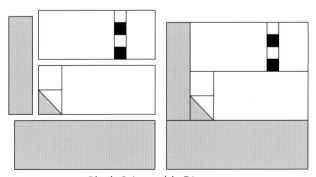

Block G Assembly Diagram

BLOCK H

Make (1) Block H using:

- (1) 2½" (6.4cm) White/Light Blue BG HST unit
- (1) 2½" (6.4cm) Blue/Light Blue BG HST unit
- (1) 2½" x 4½" (6.4cm x 11.4cm) White rectangle
- (1) 2½" x 6½" (6.4cm x 16.5cm) White rectangle
- (1) 2½" (6.4cm) Maroon square
- (2) 1" x 2½" (2.5cm x 6.4cm) Maroon rectangles
- (2) 1" x 2½" (2.5cm x 6.4cm) Yellow rectangles
- (1) 2½" (6.4cm) Black square
- (1) 2½" x 6½" (6.4cm x 16.5cm) Red rectangle
- (1) 2½" x 4½" (6.4cm x 11.4cm) Light Blue BG rectangle
- (1) 6½" (16.5) Light Blue BG square
- (1) 4½" x 12½" (11.4cm x 31.8cm) Light Blue BG rectangle

1. Referring to the Block H Assembly Diagram, join (2) 1" x 2½" (2.5cm x 6.4cm) rectangles each of Maroon and Yellow to form a strip set, alternating the colors; trim to 2½" (6.4cm) square. Sew (1) 2½" x 4½" (6.4cm x 11.4cm) White rectangle to the bottom of the Maroon/Yellow strip set and (1) 2½" (6.4cm) Maroon square to the top. Join (1) 2½" (6.4cm) White/Light Blue BG HST unit and (1) 2½" x 6½" (6.4cm x 16.5cm) White rectangle. Sew the White/Light Blue BG HST unit to the right side of the Fringe unit as shown.

2. Join (1) 2½" x 4½" (6.4cm x 11.4cm) Light Blue BG rectangle and (1) 2½" (6.4cm) Blue/Light Blue BG HST unit. Sew (1) 6½" (16.5cm) Light Blue BG square to the bottom of the unit.

3. Join (1) 2½" (6.4cm) Black square and (1) 2½" x 6½" (6.4cm x 16.5cm) Red rectangle.

5. Join the units together. Sew (1) 4½" x 12½" (11.4cm x 31.8cm) Light Blue BG rectangle to the bottom to complete the block.

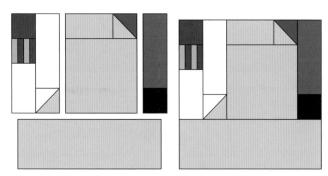

Block H Assembly Diagram

BLOCK I

Assemble (1) I Block using:

- (1) 2½" (6.4cm) Blue/Light Blue BG HST unit
- (1) 2" x 2½" (5.1cm x 6.4cm) Red rectangle (left of buttons)
- (1) 2½" x 4" (6.4cm x 10.2cm) Red rectangle (right of buttons)
- (1) 4½" x 6½" (11.4cm x 16.5cm) Red rectangle
- (1) 1½" (3.8cm) Red square
- (1) 1½" (3.9cm) Yellow square
- (1) 2½" x 6½" (6.4cm x 16.5cm) Black rectangle
- (1) 2½" x 4½" (6.4cm x 11.4cm) Light Blue BG rectangle
- (1) 6½" (16.5cm) Light Blue BG square
- (1) 4½" x 12½" (11.4cm x 31.8cm) Light Blue BG rectangle

1. Join (1) 1½" (3.8cm) square each of Yellow and Red to make a Button Column unit. Square to 1½" x 2½" (3.8cm x 6.4cm). Sew (1) 2" x 2½" (5.1cm x 6.4cm) Red rectangle to the left side of the Button Column unit and (1) 2½" x 4" (6.4cm x 10.2cm) Red rectangle to the right. Sew (1) 4½" x 6½" (11.4cm x 16.5cm) Red rectangle to the bottom of the Button Column. Then sew (1) 2½" x 6½" (6.4cm x 16.5cm) Black rectangle to the bottom of the unit as shown.

3. Join (1) 2½" (6.4cm) Blue/Light Blue BG HST unit and (1) 2½" x 4½" (6.4cm x 11.4cm) Light Blue BG rectangle. Sew (1) 6½" (16.5cm) Light Blue BG square to the bottom of the unit.

4. Join the Red/Black unit and Blue/Light Blue BG unit. Sew (1) 4½" x 12½" (11.4cm x 31.8cm) Light Blue BG rectangle to the bottom of the unit to complete the block.

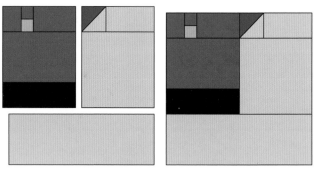

Block I Assembly Diagram

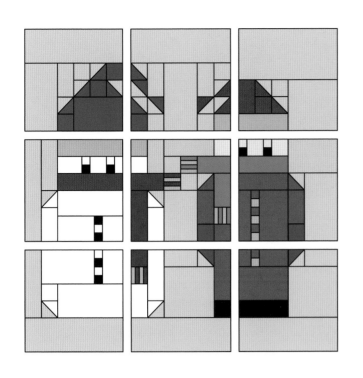

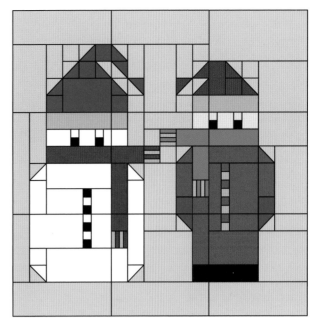

Quilt Assembly Diagram

Finish the Quilt Top

1. Referring to the Quilt Assembly Diagram, join the blocks together in rows of three as follows:

Row 1: A–C
Row 2: D–F
Row 3: G–I
Join the rows and press.

2. Sew (1) 2½" (7.6cm) x WOF border strip to the left side only. Trim to fit and press.

3. Layer the quilt top, batting, and backing; baste. Quilt as desired.

4. Bind the quilt.

Mr. Kringle

My granny was the queen of all things Santa! To help keep her tradition alive, I created this handsome fella. He always manages to stand out amongst the plethora of festive décor. This striking wall hanging is made using 12 unique blocks and a striking red-and-white border.

36" x 48" (91.4cm x 121.9cm)
Designed and quilted by Sherilyn Mortensen
Pieced by Amy Maxfield
Fabric: Kaufman Essex, V and Co. Ombre Confetti

Fabric Requirements
- ⅓ yard (0.3m) each of Red and Light Gray
- 1 yard (0.9M) Dark Red
- ⅔ yard (0.6m) White
- 5" (12.7cm) square each of Pink and Black
- ⅛ yard (0.1m) or (1) 10" square each of Beige and Gray
- ¾ yard (0.7m) Dark Gray background fabric
- 3 yards (2.7m) Backing fabric
- 15" (38.1cm) x Width of Fabric (WOF) Binding fabric

Cutting Instructions

From Red fabric (hat), cut:
- (1) 1½" (3.8cm) square
- (4) 2½" (6.4cm) squares
- (1) 2½" x 12½" (6.4cm x 31.8cm) rectangle
- (2) 4½" (11.4cm) squares
- (5) 3½" (8.9cm) squares

From Dark Red fabric (border), cut:
- (16) 2½" (6.4cm) squares
- (16) 2½" x 6½" (6.4cm x 16.5cm) rectangles
- (12) 2½" x 12½" (6.4cm x 31.8cm) rectangles
-

From White fabric (border/hat rim/pom-pom), cut:
- (20) 2½" (6.4cm) squares
- (8) 2½" x 6½" (6.4cm x 16.5cm) rectangles
- (6) 2½" x 12½" (6.4cm x 31.8cm) rectangles
- (2) 4½" (11.4cm) squares
- (1) 4½" x 12½" (11.4cm x 31.8cm) rectangle

From Pink fabric (nose/lips), cut:
- (4) 1½" (3.8cm) squares

From Beige fabric (face), cut:
- (3) 2½" (6.4cm) squares
- (2) 1½" (3.8cm) squares
- (2) 1½" x 2½" (3.8cm x 6.4cm) rectangles
- (1) 3½" (8.9cm) square

From Black fabric (eyes), cut:
- (2) 1½" (3.8cm) squares

From Gray fabric (mustache/eyebrows), cut:
- (2) 1½" x 2½" (3.8cm x 6.4cm) rectangles
- (1) 2½" x 4½" (6.4cm x 11.4cm) rectangle
- (3) 3½" (8.9cm) squares

From Light Gray fabric (beard), cut:
- (5) 2½" (6.4cm) squares
- (3) 2½" x 4½" (6.4cm x 11.4cm) rectangles
- (1) 4½" x 10½" (11.4cm x 26.7cm) rectangle
- (8) 3½" (8.9cm) squares

From Dark Gray (background) fabric, cut:
- (5) 6½" (16.5cm) squares
- (8) 2½" (6.4cm) squares
- (2) 2½" x 4½" (6.4cm x 11.4cm) rectangles
- (2) 2½" x 6½" (6.4cm x 16.5cm) rectangles
- (3) 2½" x 12½" (6.4cm x 31.8cm) rectangles
- (1) 4½" (11.4cm) square
- (1) 4½" x 10½" (11.4cm x 26.7cm) rectangle
- (1) 6½" x 8½" (16.5cm x 21.6cm) square
- (1) 6½" x 10½" (16.5cm x 26.7cm) rectangle
- (7) 1½" (3.8cm) squares
- (11) 3½" (8.9cm) squares

Assembly

1. Referring to the Half Square Triangle (HST) directions on page 8, make the following HST units from 3½" (8.9cm) squares. Press seams open and trim to 2½" (6.4cm) square.

- (9) Red/Dark Gray BG units from (5) squares each (one unit will not be used)
- (10) Light Gray/Dark Gray BG units from (5) squares each
- (2) Light Gray/Beige units from (1) square each
- (4) Light Gray/Gray units from (2) squares each
- (2) Gray/Dark Gray BG units from (1) square each

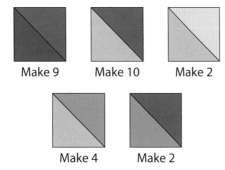

Make 9 Make 10 Make 2

Make 4 Make 2

2. Referring to the Corner Flip (CF) instructions on page 10, make the following CF units.

- (2) 2½" (6.4cm) Light Gray/Pink CF units from (2) 2½" (6.4cm) Light Gray squares and (2) 1½" (3.8cm) Pink squares, sewing a Pink square on a corner of each Light Gray square
- (2) 2½" (6.4cm) Beige/Pink CF units from (2) 2½" (6.4cm) Beige squares and (2) 1½" (3.2cm) Pink squares, sewing a pink square on one corner of each beige square.

Make 2 of Each

- (1) 4½" (11.4cm) White/Dark Gray CF unit from (1) 4½" (11.4cm) White square and (4) 1½" (3.8cm) Dark Gray squares, sewing a Dark Gray square onto each corner of the White square
- (1) 4½" (11.4cm) White/Dark Gray CF unit using (1) 4½" (11.4cm) White square and (2) 1½" (3.8cm) Dark Gray squares, sewing the dark gray squares onto the same side of the white square.

Make 1 of Each

- (1) 4½" x 12½" (11.4cm x 31.8cm) White/Red/ Dark Gray CF unit by sewing (1) 1½" (3.8cm) Red square on the upper right corner of (1) 4½" x 12½" (11.4cm x 31.8cm) White horizontal rectangle and (1) 1½" (3.8cm) Dark Gray square on the bottom right

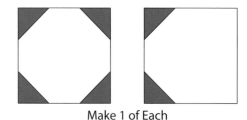

Make 1

Block Unit Assembly

Block size: 12½" (31.8cm)
Refer to the individual block assembly diagrams when making each block. Press seams, taking care to nest the seams by alternating pressing directions. Note: Seams that don't need nesting can be pressed in either direction.

BLOCK A (CORNER UNITS) (MAKE 4)
Assemble each Block A using:
- (4) 2½" (6.4cm) Dark Red squares
- (5) 2½" (6.4cm) White squares
- (4) 2½" x 6½" (6.4cm x 16.5cm) Dark Red rectangles
- (2) 2½" x 6½" (6.4cm x 16.5cm) White rectangles
- (1) 6½" (16.5cm) Dark Gray BG square

1. Join (5) 2½" (6.4cm) White squares and (4) 2½" (6.4cm) Dark Red squares to form a nine patch unit.

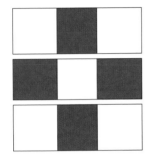

2. Join (2) 2½" x 6½" (6.4cm x 16.5cm) Dark Red rectangles and (1) 2½" x 6½" (6.4cm x 16.5cm) White rectangle, alternating the colors. Press seams open. Make 2 strip sets.

3. Referring to the Block A Assembly Diagram, join the nine patch unit, the (2) Red/White Strip sets, and (1) 6½" (16.5cm) Dark Gray BG square as shown to complete the Corner unit. Make (4) units.

Block A Assembly Diagram

BLOCK B
Assemble (1) Block B using:
- (2) 2½" (6.4cm) Red squares
- (1) 4½" (11.4cm) Red square
- (2) 2½" x 12½" (6.4cm x 31.8cm) Dark Red rectangles
- (1) 2½" x 12½" (6.4cm x 31.8cm) White rectangle
- (1) 2½" x 12½" (6.4cm x 31.8cm) Dark Gray rectangle
- (2) 2½" (6.4cm) Dark Gray squares
- (4) 2½" (6.4cm) Red/Dark Gray HST units

1. Referring to the Block B Assembly Diagram for placement and orientation, join (1) 2½" (6.4cm) Dark Gray square, (2) 2½" (6.4cm) Red/Dark Gray HST units, and (1) 2½" (6.4cm) Red square. Press seams in opposite directions. Make 2 units, noting the orientation of the HST units. Sew (1) unit to either side of (1) 4½" (11.4cm) Red square as shown.

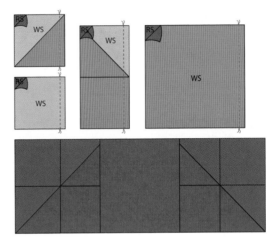

2. Join (2) 2½" x 12½" (6.4cm x 31.8cm) Dark Red rectangles and (1) 2½" x 12½" (6.4cm x 31.8cm) White rectangle, alternating the colors. Then sew (1) 2½" x 12½" (6.4cm x 31.8cm) Dark Gray rectangle to the bottom of the Red/White strip set. Join the units you just made as shown. Press the border seams open.

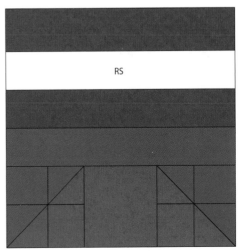

Block B Assembly Diagram

BLOCK C

Assemble (1) Block C using:

- (2) 2½" x 12½" (6.4cm x 31.8cm) Dark Red rectangles
- (1) 2½" x 12½" (6.4cm x 31.8cm) White rectangle
- (1) 2½" x 12½" (6.4cm x 31.8cm) Dark Gray BG rectangle
- (1) 2½" (6.4cm) Dark Gray BG square
- (1) 2½" x 6½" (6.4cm x 16.5cm) Dark Gray BG rectangle
- (1) 2½" x 4½" (6.4cm x 11.4cm) Light Gray rectangle
- (1) 4½" (11.4cm) White/Dark Gray BG CF unit
- (1) 2½" (6.4cm) Red/Dark Gray BG HST unit
- (1) 2½" (6.4cm) Light Gray/Dark Gray BG HST unit

1. Referring to the Block C Assembly Diagram for placement and orientation, join (1) 2½" (6.4cm) Dark Gray BG square, (1) 2½" (6.4cm) Red/Dark Gray BG HST unit, and (1) 4½" (11.4cm) White/Dark Gray BG CF unit.

2. Join (1) 2½" x 4½" (6.4cm x 11.4cm) Light Gray rectangle and (1) 2½" (6.4cm) Light Gray/Dark Gray HST unit. Sew (1) 2½" x 6½" (6.4cm x 16.5cm) Dark Gray rectangle along the left side.

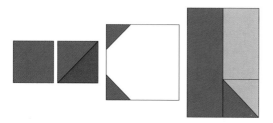

3. Join (2) 2½" x 12½" (6.4cm x 31.8cm) Dark Red rectangles, (1) 2½" x 12½" (6.4cm x 31.9cm) White rectangle, and (1) 2½" x 12½" (6.4cm x 31.8cm) Dark Gray BG rectangle in a strip set, alternating the colors as shown.

3. Referring to the Block C Assembly Diagram, join the units you just made. Press the border seams open.

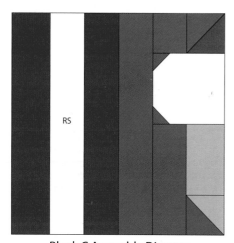

Block C Assembly Diagram

BLOCK D

Assemble (1) D block using:

- (2) 1½" (3.8cm) Beige squares
- (1) 2½" (6.4cm) Beige square
- (2) 1½" x 2½" (3.8cm x 6.4cm) Beige rectangles
- (2) 1½" x 2½" (3.8cm x 6.4cm) Gray rectangles
- (1) 2½" x 4½" (6.4cm x 11.4cm) Gray rectangle
- (1) 2½" x 4½" (6.4cm x 11.4cm) Light Gray rectangle
- (2) 1½" (3.8cm) Black squares
- (1) 2½" x 12½" (6.4cm x 31.8cm) Red rectangle
- (1) 2½" x 6½" (6.4cm x 16.5cm) Dark Gray BG rectangle
- (1) 4½" x 12½" (11.4cm x 31.8cm) White/Red/Dark Gray BG CF unit
- (2) 2½" (6.4cm) Beige/Pink CF units
- (2) 2½" (6.4cm) Light Gray/Beige HST units
- (2) 2½" (6.4cm) Light Gray/Gray HST units
- (1) 2½" (6.4cm) Light Gray/Dark Gray BG HST unit

1. Referring to the diagram, join (1) 1½" (3.8cm) square each of Beige and Black. Sew (1) 1½" x 2½" (3.8cm x 6.4cm) Gray rectangle along the top of the Beige/Black unit and (1) 1½" x 2½" (3.8cm x 6.4cm) Beige rectangle to the side facing the beige square. Make 2 eye units, noting the placement of the Beige and Black squares for the second unit.

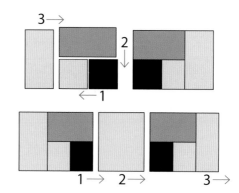

2. Referring to the Block D Assembly Diagram for placement and orientation, join the units in rows.
Row 1: (2) eye units and (1) 2½" (6.4cm) Beige square
Row 2: (2) 2½" (6.4cm) Light Gray/Beige HST units, (2) 2½" (6.4cm) Beige/Pink CF Units, noting the placement of the pink corners
Row 3: (2) 2½" (6.4cm) Light Gray/Gray HST units and (1) 2½" x 4½" (6.4cm x 11.4cm) Gray rectangle

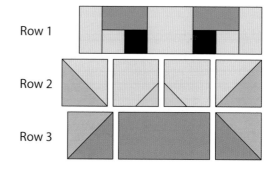

3. Join rows 1–3.

4. Sew (1) 2½" (6.4cm) Light Gray/Dark Gray HST unit to the bottom of a 2½" x 4½" (6.4cm x 11.4cm) Light Gray vertical rectangle, then join (1) 2½" x 6½" (6.4cm x 16.5cm) Dark Gray BG vertical rectangle along the right side. Join the unit to the right side of the Eye/Nose/Mustache unit.

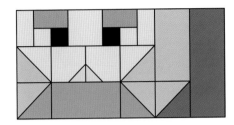

5. Join (1) 4½" x 12½" (11.4cm x 31.8cm) White/Red/Dark Gray BG CF unit and (1) 2½" x 12½" (6.4cm x 31.8cm) Red Rectangle along the top of the Eye/Nose/Mustache unit as shown to complete the block.

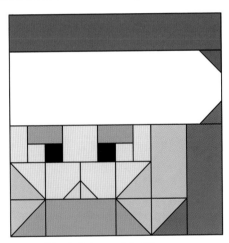

Block D Assembly Diagram

BLOCK E

Assemble (1) Block E using:
- (2) 2½" (6.4cm) Red squares
- (1) 4½" (11.4cm) Red square
- (2) 2½" (6.4cm) Dark Gray BG squares
- (2) 2½" x 12½" (6.4cm x 31.8cm) Dark Red rectangles
- (1) 2½" x 12½" (6.4cm x 31.8cm) White rectangle
- (1) 2½" x 12½" (6.4cm x 31.8cm) Dark Gray BG rectangle
- (4) 2½" (6.4cm) Red/Dark Gray BG HST units

1. Referring to the Block E Assembly Diagram for placement and orientation, join (1) 2½" (6.4cm) Red square, (2) 2½" (6.4cm) Red/Dark Gray BG HST units, and (1) 2½" (6.4cm) Dark Gray BG square to form a four patch. Make 2 four patch units. Then sew (1) Red/Dark Gray four patch unit to either side of the 4½" (11.4cm) Red square.

2. Sew the 2½" x 12½" (6.4cm x 31.8cm) rectangles in Dark Gray, Dark Red, and White to the right side of the HST unit as shown, alternating the colors, to complete the block.

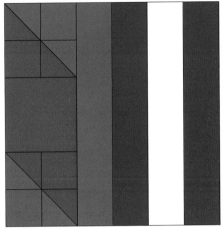

Block E Assembly Diagram

BLOCK F

Assemble (1) Block F using:
- (2) 2½" x 12½" (6.4cm x 31.8cm) Dark Red rectangles
- (1) 2½" x 12½" (6.4cm x 31.8cm) White rectangle
- (1) 2½" x 4½" (6.4cm x 11.4cm) Dark Gray BG rectangle
- (1) 6½" x 10½" (16.5cm x 26.7cm) Dark Gray BG rectangle
- (1) 2½" (6.4cm) Gray/Dark Gray BG HST unit

1. Referring to the Block F Assembly Diagram, join (1) 2½" (6.4cm) Gray/Dark Gray BG HST unit, (1) 2½" x 4½" (6.4cm x 11.4cm) Dark Gray BG rectangle, and (1) 6½" x 10½" (16.5cm x 26.7cm) Dark Gray BG rectangle.

2. Sew (2) 2½" x 12½" (6.4cm x 31.8cm) Dark Red rectangles and (1) 2½" x 12½" (6.4cm x 31.8cm) White rectangle to the left side of the Gray HST unit, alternating colors as shown.

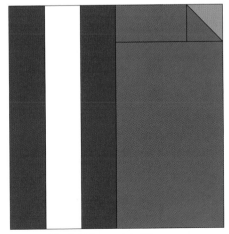

Block F Assembly Diagram

BLOCK G ASSEMBLY

Assemble (1) Block G using:

- (2) 2½" (6.4cm) Light Gray squares
- (1) 2½" x 4½" (6.4cm x 11.4cm) Light Gray rectangle
- (1) 4½" x 10½" (11.4cm x 26.7cm) Light Gray rectangle
- (1) 2½" (6.4cm) Dark Gray BG square
- (1) 4½" x 10½" (11.4cm x 26.7cm) Dark Gray BG rectangle
- (2) 2½" (6.4cm) Light Gray/Pink CF units
- (2) 2½" (6.4cm) Light Gray/Gray HST units
- (1) 2½" (6.4cm) Gray/Dark Gray BG HST unit
- (6) 2½" (6.4cm) Light Gray/Dark Gray BG HST units

1. Referring to the diagram for placement and orientation of the HST and CF units, join (2) 2½" (6.4cm) Light Gray/Gray HST units, (2) 2½" (6.4cm) Light Gray/Pink CF units, (1) 2½" (6.4cm) Gray/Dark Gray BG HST unit, and (1) 2½" (6.4cm) Dark Gray BG square.

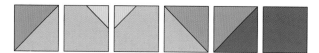

2. Referring to the Block G Assembly Diagram for placement and orientation, join the following units in columns:

Column 1: (2) 2½" (6.4cm) Light Gray squares and (3) 2½" (6.4cm) Light Gray/Dark Gray HST units

Column 2: (3) 2½" (6.4cm) Light Gray/Dark Gray HST units and (1) 2½" x 4½" (6.4cm x 11.4cm) Light Gray rectangle

3. Sew (1) 4½" x 10½" (11.4cm x 26.7cm) Light Gray rectangle to the right side of Column 1 and (1) 4½" x 10½" (11.4cm x 26.7cm) Dark Gray unit to the right side of Column 2. Join the columns, then sew the Pink/Light Gray CF unit to the top as shown to complete the block.

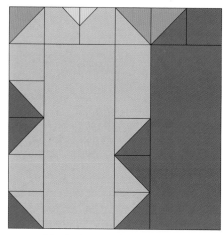

Block G Assembly Diagram

BLOCK H

Assemble (1) Block H using:

- (2) 2½" x 12½" (6.4cm x 31.8cm) Dark Red rectangles
- (1) 2½" x 12½" (6.4cm x 31.8cm) White rectangle
- (1) 2½" x 4½" (6.4cm x 11.4cm) Dark Gray BG rectangle
- (1) 6½" x 8½" (11.4 x 21.6cm) Dark Gray BG rectangle
- (1) 4½" (11.4cm) White/Dark Gray BG CF unit

1. Referring to the Block H Assembly Diagram for placement and orientation, join (1) 2½" x 4½" (6.4cm x 11.4cm) Dark Gray BG rectangle, (1) 4½" (11.4cm) White/Dark Gray BG CF unit, and (1) 6½" x 8½" (11.4 x 21.6cm) Dark Gray BG rectangle.

2. Join (2) 2½" x 12½" (6.4cm x 31.8cm) Dark Red rectangles and (1) 2½" x 12½" (6.4cm x 31.8cm) White rectangle to the right side of the White/Gray CF unit, alternating the colors as shown, to complete the block.

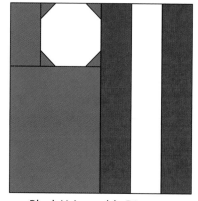

Block H Assembly Diagram

BLOCK I

Assemble (1) Block I using:

- (2) 2½" x 12½" (6.4cm x 31.8cm) Dark Red rectangles
- (1) 2½" x 12½" (6.4cm x 31.8cm) White rectangle
- (1) 2½" (6.4cm) Light Gray square
- (2) 2½" (6.4cm) Dark Gray squares
- (1) 4½" (11.4cm) Dark Gray BG square
- (1) 6½" (16.5cm) Dark Gray square
- (2) 2½" (6.4cm) Light Gray/Dark Gray HST units

1. Referring to the Block I Assembly Diagram for orientation and placement, join (1) 2½" (6.4cm) Dark Gray square, (1) 2½" (6.4cm) Light Gray/Dark Gray HST unit, and (1) 2½" (6.4cm) Light Gray square.

2. Join (1) Light Gray/Dark Gray HST unit and (1) 2½" (6.4cm) Dark Gray square as shown, then sew (1) 4½" (11.4cm) Dark Gray BG square to the left side.

3. Join the HST units, then sew (1) 6½" (16.5cm) Dark Gray square to the right side.

4. Sew (2) 2½" x 12½" (6.4cm x 31.8cm) Dark Red rectangles and (1) 2½" x 12½" (6.4cm x 31.8cm) White rectangle to the bottom of the HST unit, alternating the colors as shown, to complete the block.

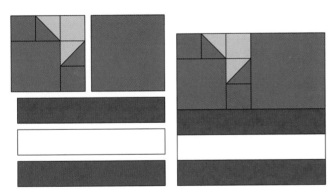

Block I Assembly Diagram

Finishing the Quilt Top

1. Referring to the Quilt Top Assembly Diagram, arrange the blocks in rows of 3 as shown.

2. Join the rows and press.

3. Layer the quilt top, batting, and backing; baste. Quilt as desired.

3. Bind the quilt.

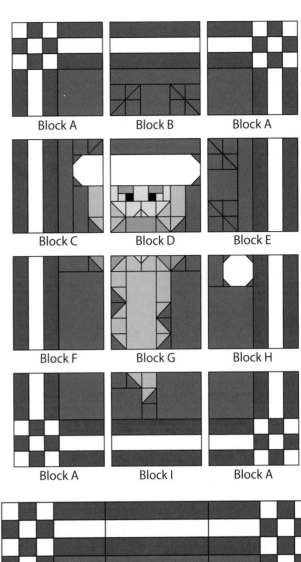

Block A   Block B   Block A

Block C   Block D   Block E

Block F   Block G   Block H

Block A   Block I   Block A

Quilt Assembly Diagram

Three Trees

My most memorable Christmas growing up was the year my dad set up our Christmas tree in the middle of the family room. It took center stage and made the holiday even more magical! This 20-block quilt is a great size for a magnificent wall hanging or a small comfortable throw that will add some magic to your holiday season.

48" x 58" (121.9cm x 147.3cm)
Designed, pieced, and quilted by Sherilyn Mortensen
Quilt bound by Amy Maxfield
Fabric: Moda Grunge, stash

Fabric Requirements

- ¾ yard (0.7m) Light Green for the left tree
- 1¼ yard (1.1m) Dark Green for the middle tree
- ¾ yard (0.7m) Green for the right tree
- ⅛ yard (0.1m) each Blue, Red, White, Bright Yellow for the lights
- ⅛ yard (0.1m) each Yellow and Dark Yellow for the stars
- 2" (5.1cm) x Width of Fabric (WOF) or (1) 10" (25.4cm) square Brown for the trunks
- 2 yards (1.8m) White background fabric
- 3½ yards (3.2m) Backing fabric
- ½ yard (0.5m) Binding fabric

Cutting Instructions

From Light Green (left tree) and Green (right tree) fabrics, cut:
- (20) 3½" (8.9cm) squares
- (68) 2½" (6.4cm) squares

From Dark Green fabric (middle tree), cut:
- (22) 3½" (8.9cm) squares
- (138) 2½" (6.4cm) squares

From Yellow and Dark Yellow fabrics (stars), cut:
- (12) 3½" (8.9cm) squares

From Bright Yellow and White fabrics, cut:
- (68) 1" (2.5cm) squares

From Blue and Red fabrics, cut:
- (69) 1" (2.5cm) squares

From Brown fabric (trunks), cut:
- (6) 1½" x 4½" (3.8cm x 11.4cm) rectangles

From White Background Fabric, cut:
- (36) 3½" (8.9cm) squares
- (2) 6½" x 12½" (16.5cm x 31.8cm) rectangles
- (6) 4½" x 12½" (11.4cm x 31.8cm) rectangles
- (8) 2½" x 4½" (6.4cm x 11.4cm) rectangles
- (16) 2½" (6.4cm) squares
- (2) 4½" (11.4cm) squares
- (2) 2½" x 12½" (6.4cm x 31.8cm) rectangles
- (6) 4½" x 6½" (11.4cm x 31.8cm) rectangles
- (2) 6½" x 8½" (16.5cm x 21.6cm) rectangles
- (2) 4½" x 8½" (11.4cm x 21.6cm) rectangles
- (2) 4½" x 9½" (11.4cm x 24.1cm) rectangles
- (2) 6½" x 11½" (31.8cm x 29.2cm) rectangles
- (4) 1½" x 2½" (3.8cm x 6.4cm) rectangles
- (2) 1½" x 6½" (3.8cm x 31.8cm) rectangles
- (2) 2½" x 6½" (6.4cm x 31.8cm) rectangles

Assembly

1. Following the Half Square Triangle (HST) instructions on page 8, make the following HST units from 3½" (8.9cm) squares. Press seams open and trim to 2½" (6.4cm) square.

- (15) Light Green/Dark Green units from (8) squares each (one will not be used)

Make 15

- (15) Dark Green/Green units from (8) squares each (one unit will not be used)

Make 15

- (21) Light Green/White (BG) units from (11) squares each (one will not be used)

Make 21

- (10) Dark Green/White (BG) units from (5) squares each

Make 10

- (21) Green/White BG units from (11) squares each (one will not be used)

Make 21

- (2) Dark Green/Dark Yellow units from (1) square each

Make 2

- (2) Green/Yellow units from (1) square each
- (2) Light Green/Yellow units from (1) square each
- (8) Yellow/White (BG) units from (4) squares each
- (10) Dark Yellow/White (BG) units from (5) squares each
- (12) Yellow/Dark Yellow units from (6) squares each

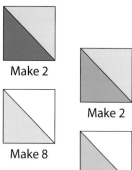

Make 2

Make 2

Make 8

Make 10

Make 12

2. Following the Corner Flip (CF) unit instructions on page 10, make the following CF units. Press seams open.

- (68) Light Green CF units from (68) 2½" (6.4cm) Light Green squares and (17) 1" (2.5cm) squares each in Blue, Red, Bright Yellow, and White, sewing the smaller square in one corner of each Light Green square for the Light Green (Left) Tree

Make 17

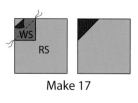

Make 17   Make 17   Make 17

- (138) 2½" (6.4cm) Dark Green CF units from (138) 2½" (6.4cm) Dark Green squares and (35) 1" (2.5cm) squares each in Blue and Red and (34) 1" (2.5cm) squares each in Bright Yellow and White, sewing (1) smaller square on one corner of each Dark Green square for the Dark Green (Middle) Tree

Make 35   Make 35   Make 34   Make 34

- (68) Green CF units from (68) 2½" (6.4cm) Green squares and (17) 1" (2.5cm) squares each in Blue, Red, Bright Yellow, and White, sewing the smaller square in one corner of each Green square for the Green (Right) Tree

Make 17   Make 17   Make 17   Make 17

Block Assembly

Refer to the individual Block Diagrams throughout assembly, noting the orientation of the HST and CF units. Press the seams, taking care to nest seams by alternating pressing directions.

BLOCK A ASSEMBLY

Block size: 10½" x 12½" (26.7cm x 31.8cm) (Make 1)
Assemble A block using:

- (1) 2½" (6.4cm) Yellow/Dark Yellow HST unit
- (1) 2½" (6.4cm) Dark Yellow/White (BG) HST unit
- (1) 2½" (6.4cm) Yellow/White (BG) HST unit
- (1) 2½" (6.4cm) White (BG) square
- (1) 4½" x 8½" (11.4cm x 21.6cm) White (BG) rectangle to the left of the unit
- (1) 6½" x 12½" (16.5cm x 31.8cm) White (BG) rectangle

1. Join (1) 2½" (6.4cm) Yellow/Dark Yellow HST unit, (1) 2½" (6.4cm) Dark Yellow/White (BG) HST unit, (1) 2½" (6.4cm) Yellow/White (BG) HST unit, and (1) 2½" (6.4cm) White (BG) square in a four patch as show. Sew (1) 4½" x 8½" (11.4cm x 21.6cm) White (BG) rectangle to the left side and (1) 6½" x 12½" (16.5cm x 31.8cm) White (BG) rectangle along the top to complete the block.

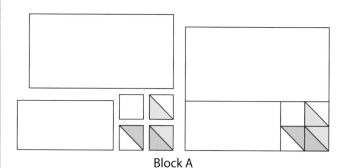

Block A

BLOCK B ASSEMBLY

Block size: 10½" x 12½" (26.7cm x 31.8cm) (Make 1)

- (3) 2½" (6.4cm) Yellow/Dark Yellow HST units
- (2) 2½" (6.4cm) Dark Yellow/White (BG) HST unit
- (3) 2½" (6.4cm) Yellow/White (BG) HST units
- (2) 2½" (6.4cm) White (BG) squares
- (1) 2½" x 4½" (6.4cm x 11.4cm) White (BG) rectangle
- (1) 4½" x 6½" (11.4cm x 16.5cm) White (BG) rectangle
- (1) 4½" x 12½" (11.4cm x 31.8cm) White (BG) rectangle

1. Join (1) 2½" (6.4cm) Yellow/Dark Yellow HST unit, (1) 2½" (6.4cm) Dark Yellow/White (BG) HST unit, (1) 2½" (6.4cm) Yellow/White (BG) HST unit, and (1) 2½" (6.4cm) White (BG) square in a four patch as shown. Sew (1) 2½" x 4½" (6.4cm x 11.4cm) White (BG) rectangle to the top of the unit.

2. Join (1) 2½" (6.4cm) White (BG) square and (2) 2½" (6.4cm) Yellow/White (BG) HST units. Then join (2) 2½" (6.4cm) Yellow/Dark Yellow HST units and (1) 2½" (6.4cm) Dark Yellow/White (BG) HST unit in a column. Join the columns. Referring to the Block A Diagram, sew (1) HST unit to the left side of (1) 4½" x 6½" (11.4cm x 16.5cm) White (BG) rectangle and (1) HST unit to the right. Sew (1) 4½" x 12½" (11.4cm x 31.8cm) White (BG) rectangle to the top to complete the block.

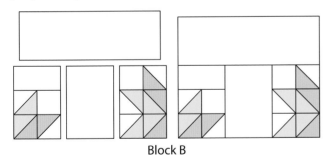

Block B

BLOCK C ASSEMBLY

Block size: 10½" x 12½" (26.7cm x 31.8cm) (Make 1)
Assemble (1) C block using:

- (3) 2½" (6.4cm) Yellow/Dark Yellow HST units
- (3) 2½" (6.4cm) Yellow/White (BG) HST units
- (2) 2½" (6.4cm) Dark Yellow/White (BG) HST units
- (1) 4½" x 12½" (11.4cm x 31.8cm) White (BG) rectangle
- (1) 4½" x 6½" (11.4cm x 16.5cm) White (BG) rectangle
- (1) 2½" x 4½" (6.4cm x 11.4cm) White (BG) rectangle
- (2) 2½" (6.4cm) White (BG) squares

1. Referring to the Block C diagram for placement and orientation, join (1) 2½" (6.4cm) Yellow/Dark Yellow HST unit, (1) 2½" (6.4cm) Dark Yellow/White (BG) HST unit, (1) 2½" (6.4cm) Yellow/White (BG) HST unit, and (1) 2½" (6.4cm) White (BG) square in a four patch as shown. Sew (1) 2½" x 4½" (6.4cm x 11.4cm) White (BG) rectangle to the top of the unit.

2. Referring to the diagram for placement and orientation, join (2) 2½" (6.4cm) Yellow/Dark Yellow HST units and (1) 2½" (6.4cm) Dark Yellow/White (BG) HST unit in a column. Join (2) 2½" (6.4cm) Yellow/White (BG) HST units and (1) 2½" (6.4cm) White (BG) square as shown. Join the columns.

3. Join the units you just made to either side of (1) 4½" x 6½" (11.4cm x 16.5cm) White (BG) rectangle as shown. Sew (1) 4½" x 12½" (11.4cm x 31.8cm) White (BG) rectangle along the top.

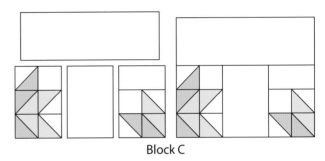

Block C

BLOCK D ASSEMBLY

Block size: 10½" x 12½" (26.7cm x 31.8cm) (Make 1)
Assemble (1) D block using:

- (1) 2½" (6.4cm) Yellow/Dark Yellow HST unit
- (1) 2½" (6.4cm) Dark Yellow/White BG HST unit
- (1) 2½" (6.4cm) Yellow/White BG HST unit
- (1) 6½" x 12½" (16.5cm x 31.8cm) White (BG) rectangle
- (1) 4½" x 8½" (11.4cm x 21.6cm) White (BG) rectangle
- (1) 2½" (6.4cm) White (BG) square

1. Join (1) 2½" (6.4cm) White (BG) square, (1) 2½" (6.4cm) Yellow/Dark Yellow HST unit, (1) 2½" (6.4cm) Dark Yellow/White BG HST unit, and (1) 2½" (6.4cm) Yellow/White BG HST unit in a four patch as shown. Sew (1) 4½" x 8½" (11.4cm x 21.6cm) White (BG) rectangle to the right of the four patch, then join (1) 4½" x 12½" (11.4cm x 31.8cm) White (BG) rectangle along the top.

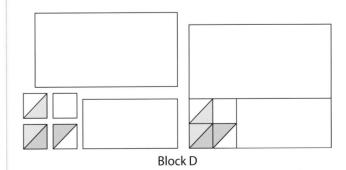

Block D

BLOCK E ASSEMBLY

Block size: 12½" (31.8cm)

Assemble (1) E block using:

- (1) 2½" (6.4cm) Yellow/Dark Yellow HST unit
- (1) 2½" (6.4cm) Dark Yellow/White BG HST unit
- (1) 2½" (6.4cm) Yellow/Light Green HST unit
- (5) 2½" (6.4cm) Light Green/White (BG) HST units
- (8) 2½" (6.4cm) Light Green CF units in a variety of colors
- (1) 6½" x 8½" (16.5cm x 21.6cm) White (BG) rectangle
- (1) 4½" x 6½" (11.4cm x 16.5cm) White (BG) rectangle
- (1) 2½" x 4½" (6.4cm x 11.4cm) White (BG) rectangle

1. Join (1) 2½" (6.4cm) Light Green/White (BG) HST unit and (1) 2½" x 4½" (6.4cm x 11.4cm) White (BG) rectangle as shown. Sew (1) (1) 4½" x 6½" (11.4cm x 16.5cm) White (BG) rectangle along the top.

2. Join (1) 2½" (6.4cm) Light Green CF unit and (2) 2½" (6.4cm) Light Green/White (BG) HST units as shown. Sew the CF unit to the right side of the Unit you just made. Sew (1) 6½" x 8½" (16.5cm x 21.6cm) White (BG) rectangle to the top.

3. Referring to the Block E diagram for placement and orientation, join the following units in columns:

Column 1: (3) 2½" (6.4cm) Light Green CF units in a variety of colors, (2) 2½" (6.4cm) Light Green/White (BG) HST units, and (1) 2½" (6.4cm) Dark Yellow/White (BG) HST unit

Column 2: (4) 2½" (6.4cm) Light Green CF units in a variety of colors, (1) 2½" (6.4cm) Yellow/Light Green HST unit, and (1) 2½" (6.4cm) Yellow/Dark Yellow HST unit

4. Sew the units together as shown to complete the block.

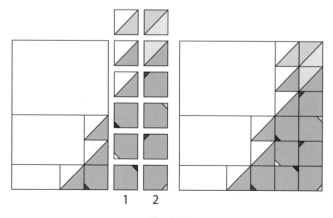

Block E

BLOCK F ASSEMBLY

Block size: 12½" (31.8cm)

Assemble (1) F block using:

- (1) 2½" (6.4cm) Yellow/Dark Yellow HST unit
- (1) 2½" (6.4cm) Dark Yellow/White (BG) HST unit
- (1) 2½" (6.4cm) Dark Yellow/Dark Green HST unit
- (1) 2½" (6.4cm) Yellow/Light Green HST unit
- (3) 2½" (6.4cm) Light Green/White (BG) HST units
- (2) 2½" (6.4cm) Light Green/Dark Green HST units
- (4) 2½" (6.4cm) Dark Green/White (BG) HST units
- (7) 2½" (6.4cm) Light Green CF units in a variety of colors
- (11) 2½" (6.4cm) Dark Green CF units in a variety of colors
- (1) 2½" x 4½" (6.4cm x 11.4cm) White (BG) rectangle
- (1) 2½" x 4½" (6.4cm x 11.4cm) White (BG) rectangle

1. Referring to the Block F diagram for placement and orientation, join the following units together in columns.

Column 1: (4) 2½" (6.4cm) Light Green CF units, (1) 2½" (6.4cm) Yellow/Light Green HST unit, and (1) 2½" (6.4cm) Yellow/Dark Yellow HST unit

Column 2: (3) 2½" (6.4cm) Light Green CF units, (2) 2½" (6.4cm) Light Green/White (BG) HST units, and (1) 2½" (6.4cm) Dark Yellow/White (BG) HST unit

Column 3: (2) 2½" (6.4cm) Light Green/Dark Green HST units, (1) 2½" (6.4cm) Light Green/White (BG) HST unit, and (1) 2½" x 6½" (6.4cm x 16.5cm) White (BG) rectangle

Column 4: (2) 2½" (6.4cm) Dark Green CF units, (2) 2½" (6.4cm) Dark Green/White (BG) HST units, and (1) 2½" x 4½" (6.4cm x 11.4cm) White (BG) rectangle

Column 5: (4) 2½" (6.4cm) Dark Green CF units and (2) 2½" (6.4cm) Dark Green/White (BG) HST units

Column 6: (5) 2½" (6.4cm) Dark Green CF units and (1) 2½" (6.4cm) Dark Yellow/Dark Green HST unit

2. Join the columns.

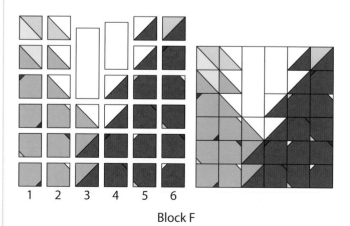

Block F

BLOCK G ASSEMBLY

Block size: 12½" (31.8cm)

Make (1) block using:

- (1) 2½" (6.4cm) Yellow/Dark Yellow HST unit
- (1) 2½" (6.4cm) Dark Yellow/White BG HST unit
- (1) 2½" (6.4cm) Dark Yellow/Dark Green HST unit
- (1) 2½" (6.4cm) Yellow/Green HST unit
- (3) 2½" (6.4cm) Green/White BG HST units
- (2) 2½" (6.4cm) Dark Green/Green HST units
- (4) 2½" (6.4cm) Dark Green/White BG HST units
- (11) 2½" (6.4cm) Dark Green CF units in a variety of colors
- (7) 2½" (6.4cm) Green CF units in a variety of colors
- (1) 2½" x 4½" (6.4cm x 11.4cm) White (BG) rectangle
- (1) 2½" x 6½" (6.4cm x 16.5cm) White (BG) rectangle

1. Referring to the Block G diagram for placement and orientation, join the following units in columns.

Column 1: (5) 2½" (6.4cm) Dark Green CF units and (1) 2½" (6.4cm) Dark Yellow/Dark Green HST unit

Column 2: (4) 2½" (6.4cm) Dark Green CF units and (2) 2½" (6.4cm) Dark Green/White (BG) HST units

Column 3: (2) 2½" (6.4cm) Dark Green CF units, (2) 2½" (6.4cm) Dark Green/White (BG) HST units, and (1) 2½" x 4½" (6.4cm x 11.4cm) White (BG) rectangle

Column 4: (2) 2½" (6.4cm) Green/Dark Green HST units, (1) 2½" (6.4cm) Green/White (BG) HST unit, and (1) 2½" x 6½" (6.4cm x 16.5cm) White (BG) rectangle

Column 5: (3) 2½" (6.4cm) Green CF units, (2) 2½" (6.4cm) Green/White (BG) HST units, and (1) 2½" (6.4cm) Dark Yellow/White (BG) HST unit

Column 6: (4) 2½" (6.4cm) Green CF units, (1) 2½" (6.4cm) Yellow/Green HST unit, and (1) 2½" (6.4cm) Yellow/Dark Yellow HST unit

2. Join the columns.

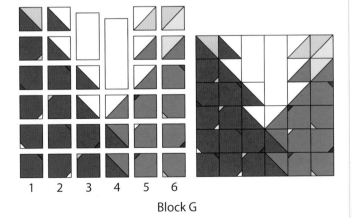

1   2   3   4   5   6

Block G

BLOCK H ASSEMBLY

Block size: 12½" (31.8cm)

Make (1) block using:

- (1) 2½" (6.4cm) Yellow/Dark Yellow HST unit
- (1) 2½" (6.4cm) Dark Yellow/White (BG) HST unit
- (1) 2½" (6.4cm) Yellow/Green HST unit
- (5) 2½" (6.4cm) Green/White (BG) HST units
- (8) 2½" (6.4cm) Green CF units in a variety of colors
- (1) 6½" x 8½" (16.5cm x 21.6cm) White (BG) rectangle
- (1) 4½" x 6½" (11.4cm x 16.5cm) White (BG) rectangle
- (1) 2½" x 4½" (6.4cm x 11.4cm) White (BG) rectangle

1. Sew (1) 2½" (6.4cm) Green/White (BG) HST unit to the left side of (1) 2½" x 4½" (6.4cm x 11.4cm) White (BG) rectangle. Sew (1) 4½" x 6½" (11.4cm x 16.5cm) White (BG) rectangle along the top.

2. Referring to the Block H diagram for placement and orientation, join (1) 2½" (6.4cm) Green CF unit and (2) 2½" (6.4cm) Green/White (BG) HST units.

3. Join the units you just made as shown. Sew (1) 6½" x 8½" (16.5cm x 21.6cm) White (BG) rectangle along the top.

3. Referring to the diagram for placement, join the following units in columns:

Column 1: (4) 2½" (6.4cm) Green CF units, (1) 2½" (6.4cm) Yellow/Green HST unit, and (1) 2½" (6.4cm) Yellow/Dark Yellow HST unit

Column 2: (3) 2½" (6.4cm) Green CF units, (2) 2½" (6.4cm) Green/White (BG) HST units, and (1) 2½" (6.4cm) Dark Yellow/White (BG) HST unit

4. Join the Columns, then sew them to the left side of the White/Green HST unit to complete the block.

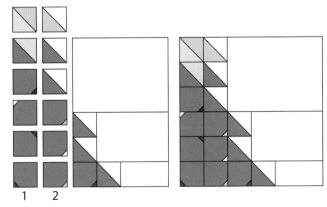

1   2

Block H

BLOCK I ASSEMBLY

Block size: 12½" (31.8cm)

Make (1) block using:

- (6) 2½" (6.4cm) Light Green/White BG HST units
- (19) 2½" (6.4cm) Light Green CF units in a variety of colors
- (1) 2½" (6.4cm) White (BG) square
- (1) 4½" (11.4cm) White (BG) square
- (1) 4½" x 6½" (11.4cm x 16.5cm) White (BG) rectangle

1. Join (1) 2½" (6.4cm) White (BG) square and (1) 2½" (6.4cm) Light Green/White BG HST unit as shown in the Block I Assembly Diagram. Sew (1) 4½" x 6½" (11.4cm x 16.5cm) White (BG) vertical rectangle to the top of the HST unit and (1) 4½" (11.4cm) White (BG) square to the bottom.

2. Referring to the Block I diagram for placement and orientation, join the following units in rows:
Column 1: (5) 2½" (6.4cm) Light Green/White BG HST units and (1) 2½" (6.4cm) Light Green CF unit
Columns 2–4: Join (6) 2½" (6.4cm) Light Green CF units

3. Join the columns. Then sew the White (BG)/Green unit to the left side of the CF units to complete the block.

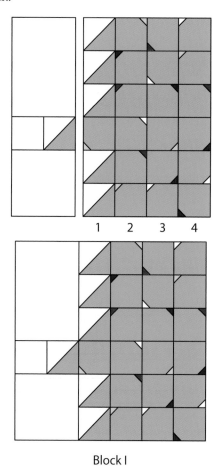

Block I

BLOCK J ASSEMBLY

Block size: 12½" (31.8cm)

Make (1) block using:

- (6) 2½" (6.4cm) Light Green/Dark Green HST units
- (5) 2½" (6.4cm) Light Green CF units in a variety of colors
- (25) 2½" (6.4cm) Dark Green CF units in a variety of colors

1. Referring to the Block J diagram for placement and orientation, join the units in columns as follows:
Column 1: (5) 2½" (6.4cm) Light Green CF units and (1) 2½" (6.4cm) Light Green/Dark Green HST unit
Column 2: (5) 2½" (6.4cm) Light Green/Dark Green HST units and (1) 2½" (6.4cm) Dark Green CF unit
Columns 3-6: (6) 2½" (6.4cm) Dark Green CF units

2. Join the rows to complete the block.

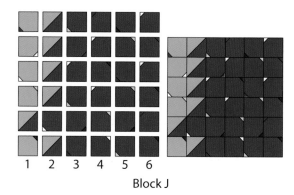

Block J

BLOCK K ASSEMBLY

Block size: 12½" (31.8cm)

Make (1) block using:

- (6) 2½" (6.4cm) Dark Green/Green HST units
- (5) 2½" (6.4cm) Green CF units in a variety of colors
- (25) 2½" (6.4cm) Dark Green CF units in a variety of colors

1. Join the units in columns as follows:
Columns 1–4: (6) 2½" (6.4cm) Dark Green CF units
Column 5: (5) 2½" (6.4cm) Green/Dark Green HST units and (1) 2½" (6.4cm) Dark Green CF unit
Column 6: (5) 2½" (6.4cm) Green CF units and (1) 2½" (6.4cm) Green/Dark Green HST unit

2. Join the columns to complete the block.

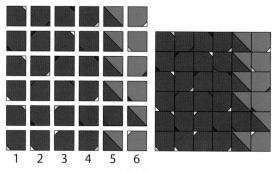

Block K

BLOCK L ASSEMBLY
Block size: 12½" (31.8cm)
Make (1) block using:
- (6) 2½" (6.4cm) Green/White (BG) HST units
- (19) 2½" (6.4cm) Green CF units in a variety of colors
- (1) 2½" (6.4cm) White (BG) square
- (1) 4½" (11.4cm) White (BG) square rectangle
- (1) 4½" x 6½" (11.4cm x 16.5cm) White (BG) rectangle

1. (1) 2½" (6.4cm) White (BG) square and (1) 2½" (6.4cm) Green/White (BG) HST unit. Sew (1) 4½" (11.4cm) White (BG) square rectangle to the bottom and (1) 4½" x 6½" (11.4cm x 16.5cm) White (BG) vertical rectangle to the top.

2. Referring to the Block L diagram for placement and orientation, join the following units in columns:
Columns 1–3: Join (6) 2½" (6.4cm) Green CF units
Column 4: Join (5) 2½" (6.4cm) Green/White (BG) HST units and (1) 2½" (6.4cm) Green CF unit

3. Join the columns. Join the units you just made as shown to complete the block.

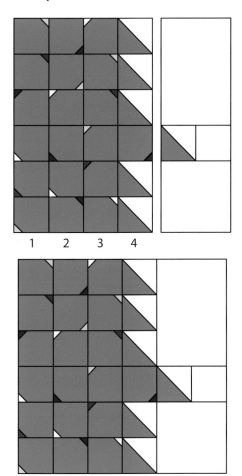

Block L

BLOCK M ASSEMBLY
Block size: 12½" (31.8cm)
Make (1) block using:
- (6) 2½" (6.4cm) Light Green/White (BG) HST units
- (20) 2½" (6.4cm) Light Green CF units in a variety of colors
- (2) 2½" (6.4cm) White (BG) squares
- (1) 2½" x 4½" (6.4cm x 11.4cm) White (BG) rectangle
- (1) 2½" x 12½" (6.4cm x 31.8cm) White (BG) rectangle

1. Referring to the Block M diagram for placement and orientation, join the units in columns as follows:
Column 1: (1) 2½" x 4½" (6.4cm x 11.4cm) White (BG) rectangle, (2) 2½" (6.4cm) White (BG) squares, and (2) 2½" (6.4cm) Light Green/White (BG) HST units
Column 2: (4) 2½" (6.4cm) Light Green/White (BG) HST units and (2) 2½" (6.4cm) Light Green CF units
Columns 3–5: (6) 2½" (6.4cm) Light Green CF units

2. Join the columns as shown. Sew (1) 2½" x 12½" (6.4cm x 31.8cm) White (BG) rectangle along the left side to complete the block.

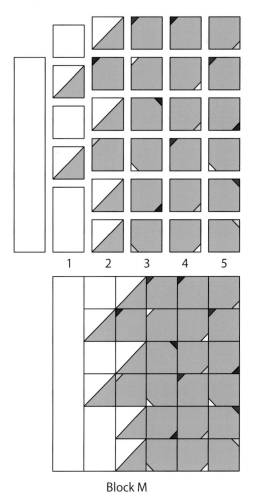

Block M

BLOCK N ASSEMBLY

Block size: 12½" (31.8cm)

Make (1) block using:
- (6) 2½" (6.4cm) Light Green/Dark Green HST units
- (4) 2½" (6.4cm) Light Green CF units in a variety of colors
- (26) 2½" (6.4cm) Dark Green CF units in a variety of colors

1. Referring to the Block N diagram for placement and orientation, join the units in columns as follows:
Column 1: (4) 2½" (6.4cm) Light Green CF units and (2) 2½" (6.4cm) Light Green/Dark Green HST units
Column 2: (4) 2½" (6.4cm) Light Green/Dark Green HST units and (2) 2½" (6.4cm) Dark Green CF units
Columns 3–6: (6) 2½" (6.4cm) Dark Green CF units

2. Join the columns as shown to complete the block.

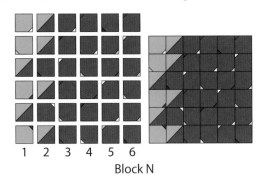

Block N

BLOCK O ASSEMBLY

Block size: 12½" (31.8cm)

Make (1) block using:
- (6) 2½" (6.4cm) Dark Green/Green HST units
- (4) 2½" (6.4cm) Green CF units in a variety of colors
- (26) 2½" (6.4cm) Dark Green CF units in a variety of colors

1. Referring to the Block O diagram for placement and orientation, join the columns as follows:
Columns 1–4: (6) 2½" (6.4cm) Dark Green CF units
Column 5: (4) 2½" (6.4cm) Dark Green/Green HST units and (2) 2½" (6.4cm) Dark Green CF units
Column 6: (4) 2½" (6.4cm) Green CF units and (2) 2½" (6.4cm) Dark Green/Green HST units

2. Join the columns to complete the block.

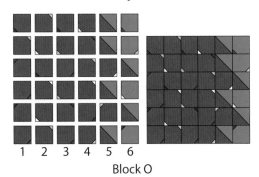

Block O

BLOCK P ASSEMBLY

Block size: 12½" (31.8cm)

Make (1) block using:
- (6) 2½" (6.4cm) Green/White (BG) HST units
- (20) 2½" (6.4cm) variety of Green CF units in a variety of colors
- (2) 2½" (6.4cm) White (BG) squares
- (1) 2½" x 4½" (6.4cm x 114cm) White (BG) rectangle
- (1) 2½" x 12½" (6.4cm x 31.8cm) White (BG) rectangle

1. Referring to the Block P diagram for placement for placement and orientation, join the units in columns as follows:
Columns 1–3: (6) 2½" (6.4cm) Green CF units
Column 4: (4) 2½" (6.4cm) Green/White (BG) HST units and (2) 2½" (6.4cm) Green CF units
Column 5: (1) 2½" x 4½" (6.4cm x 11.4cm) White (BG) rectangle, (2) 2½" (6.4cm) White (BG) squares, and (2) 2½" (6.4cm) Green/White (BG) HST units

2. Join the columns. Sew (1) 2½" x 12½" (6.4cm x 31.8cm) White (BG) rectangle to the right side of the unit to complete the block.

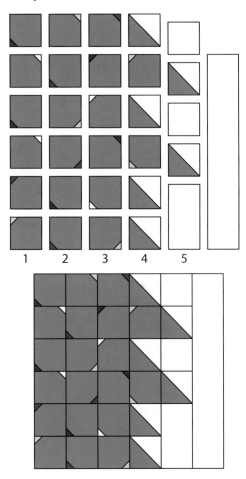

Block P

BLOCK Q ASSEMBLY

Block size: 12½" (31.8cm)

Make (1) block using:

- (1) 2½" (6.4cm) Light Green/White (BG) HST unit
- (4) 2½" (6.4cm) Light Green CF units in a variety of colors
- (1) 2½" (6.4cm) White (BG) square
- (1) 1½" x 2½" (3.8cm x 6.4cm) White (BG) rectangle
- (1) 6½" x 11½" (16.5cm x 29.2cm) White (BG) rectangle
- (1) 4½" x 12½" (11.4cm x 31.8cm) White (BG) rectangle
- (1) 1½" x 4½" (3.8cm x 6.4cm) Brown rectangle

1. Referring to the Block Q diagram for placement and orientation, join (1) 2½" (6.4cm) White (BG) square, (1) 2½" (6.4cm) Light Green/White (BG) HST unit, and (4) 2½" (6.4cm) Light Green CF units.

2. Join (1) 1½" x 2½" (3.8cm x 6.4cm) White (BG) rectangle and (1) 1½" x 4½" (3.8cm x 11.4cm) Brown rectangle as shown. Sew the unit to the right side of (1) 6½" x 11½" (16.5cm x 29.2cm) White (BG) rectangle. Sew (1) 4½" x 12½" (11.4cm x 31.8cm) White (BG) rectangle to the bottom of the unit.

3. Join the units as shown to complete the block.

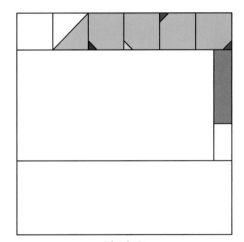

Block Q

BLOCK R ASSEMBLY

Block size: 12½" (31.8cm)

Make (1) block using:

- (1) 2½" (6.4cm) Light Green/Dark Green HST unit
- (1) 2½" (6.4cm) Dark Green/White (BG) HST unit
- (1) 2½" (6.4cm) Light Green CF unit
- (7) 2½" (6.4cm) Dark Green CF units in a variety of colors
- (1) 2½" (6.4cm) White (BG) square
- (1) 1½" x 2½" (3.8cm x 6.4cm) White (BG) rectangle
- (1) 1½" x 6½" (3.8cm x 16.5cm) White (BG) rectangle
- (1) 4½" x 9½" (11.4cm x 24.1cm) White (BG) rectangle
- (1) 4½" x 12½" (11.4cm x 31.8cm) White (BG) rectangle
- (2) 1½" x 4½" (3.8cm x 11.4cm) Brown rectangles

1. Join (1) 1½" x 2½" (3.8cm x 6.4cm) White (BG) rectangle and (1) 1½" x 4½" (3.8cm x 11.4cm) Brown rectangle. Sew (1) 1½" x 6½" (3.8cm x 16.5cm) White (BG) rectangle to the right side, then sew (1) 2½" (6.4cm) Light Green square to the top.

2. Referring to the Block R diagram for placement and orientation, join the following units in rows:
Row 1: (1) 2½" (6.4cm) Light Green/Dark Green HST unit and (4) 2½" (6.4cm) Dark Green CF units
Row 2: (1) 2½" (6.4cm) White (BG) square, (1) 2½" (6.4cm) Dark Green/White (BG) HST unit, and (3) 2½" (6.4cm) Dark Green CF units

3. Join (1) 4½" x 9½" (11.4m x 24.1cm) White (BG) rectangle and (1) 1½" x 4½" (3.8cm x 11.4cm) Brown rectangle.

4. Join the units you just made as shown. Sew (1) 4½" x 12½" (11.4cm x 31.8cm) White (BG) rectangle along the bottom to complete the block.

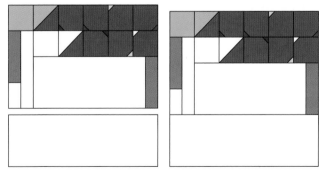

Block R

BLOCK S ASSEMBLY
Block size: 12½" (31.8cm)
Make (1) block using:
- (1) 2½" (6.4cm) Dark Green/Green HST unit
- (1) 2½" (6.4cm) Dark Green/White (BG) HST unit
- (1) 2½" (6.4cm) Green CF unit
- (7) 2½" (6.4cm) Dark Green CF units in a variety of colors
- (1) 2½" (6.4cm) White (BG) square
- (1) 1½" x 2½" (3.8cm x 6.4cm) White (BG) rectangle
- (1) 1½" x 6½" (3.8cm x 16.5cm) White (BG) rectangle
- (1) 4½" x 9½" (11.4cm x 24.1cm) White (BG) rectangle
- (1) 4½" x 12½" (6.4cm x 31.8cm) White (BG) rectangle
- (2) 1½" x 4½" (3.8cm x 6.4cm) Brown rectangles

1. Join (1) 1½" x 2½" (3.8cm x 6.4cm) White (BG) rectangle and (1) 1½" x 4½" (3.8cm x 11.4cm) Brown rectangle. Sew (1) 1½" x 6½" (3.8cm x 11.4cm) White (BG) rectangle to the left side of the unit, then sew (1) 2½" (6.4cm) Green CF unit to the top.

2. Referring to the Block S Assembly Diagram for placement and orientation, join the following units in rows:
Row 1: (4) 2½" (6.4cm) Dark Green CF units and (1) 2½" (6.4cm) Dark Green/Green HST unit
Row 2: (3) 2½" (6.4cm) Dark Green CF units, (1) 2½" (6.4cm) Dark Green/White HST unit, and (1) 2½" (6.4cm) White (BG) square

3. Sew 1½" x 4½" (3.8cm x 11.4cm) Brown rectangle to the left side of (1) 4½" x 9½" (11.4cm x 24.1cm) White (BG) rectangle.

4. Join the units you just made as shown, then sew (1) 4½" x 12½" (11.4cm x 31.8cm) White (BG) rectangle along the bottom to complete the block.

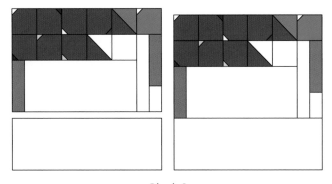

Block S

BLOCK T ASSEMBLY
Block size: 12½" (31.8cm)
Make (1) block using:
- (1) 2½" (6.4cm) Green/White BG HST unit
- (4) 2½" (6.4cm) Green CF units in a variety of colors
- (1) 2½" (6.4cm) White (BG) square
- (1) 1½" x 2½" (3.8cm x 6.4cm) White (BG) rectangle
- (1) 6½" x 11½" (16.5cm x 29.2cm) White (BG) rectangle
- (1) 4½" x 12½" (11.4cm x 31.8cm) White (BG) rectangle
- (1) 1½" x 4½" (3.8cm x 11.4cm) Brown rectangle

1. Referring to the Block T diagram for placement and orientation, join (4) 2½" (6.4cm) Green CF units, (1) 2½" (6.4cm) Green/BG HST unit, and (1) 2½" (6.4cm) White (BG) square.

2. Join (1) 1½" x 4½" (3.8cm x 11.4cm) Brown rectangle and (1) 1½" x 2½" (3.8cm x 6.4cm) White (BG) rectangle as shown. Sew the unit to the left side of (1) 6½" x 11½" (16.5cm x 29.2cm) White (BG) rectangle. Sew the Green/White CF unit row to the top and (1) 4½" x 12½" (11.4cm x 31.8cm) White (BG) rectangle to the bottom to complete the block.

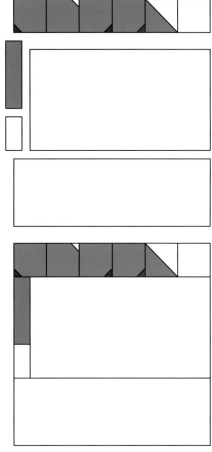

Block T

Finishing the Quilt Top

1. Referring to the Quilt Assembly Diagram, join the blocks in rows of 4 in alphabetical order. Then join the rows.

2. Layer the quilt top, batting, and backing; baste. Quilt as desired.

3. Bind the quilt.

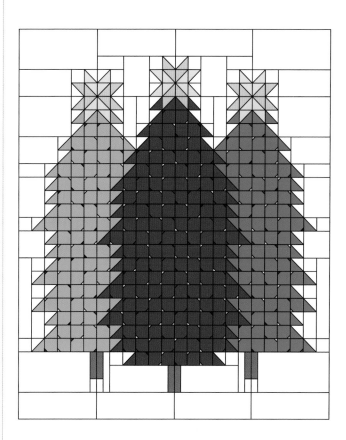

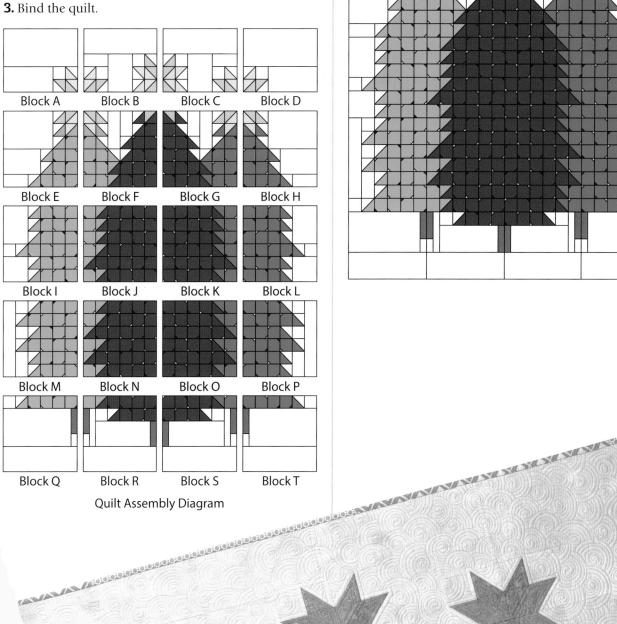

Block A   Block B   Block C   Block D

Block E   Block F   Block G   Block H

Block I   Block J   Block K   Block L

Block M   Block N   Block O   Block P

Block Q   Block R   Block S   Block T

Quilt Assembly Diagram

About the Author

Sherilyn Mortensen is the proud owner of Sea Sherilyn Sew. She is a pattern designer, teacher, presenter, and long-arm custom quilter. She is a quilt artist for Gammill and thoroughly enjoys her association with them. As a self-taught quilter, Sherilyn has improved and fine-tuned her skills throughout the years. Her passion for quilting began about 25 years ago. After gathering up some old clothes and scraps of fabric, she cut up a bunch of squares and pieced together a large king-sized quilt. Although it was not perfect, she loved it and knew her love affair with quilting had begun. To this day she still enjoys the entire quilt-making process, from the first steps of designing to the last steps of quilting. Whether quilting with others, for others, or for herself, quilting will always be one of Sherilyn's greatest joys and pleasures in life, and it has definitely been one of the best forms of therapy! Her love and passion for quilting is equally shared with her joy of being a wife, mom, gramma, daughter, sister, and friend!

Index